I0170006

THE AGE OF APOSTOLIC APOSTLESHIP SERIES

A postles and the PART 2
Local Church

On Behalf of

Connecting for Excellence
International Apostolic Network

CHURCHES AND MINISTRIES IN ASSOCIATION

By Dr. Alan Pateman

By Dr. Jennifer Pateman

Available from APMI Publications, Amazon.com and Other Retail Outlets

THE AGE OF APOSTOLIC APOSTLESHIP SERIES

Apostles PART 2 and the Local Church

DR. ALAN PATEMAN

BOOK TITLE: Apostles and the Local Church
(The Age of Apostolic Apostleship Series) Part Two

WRITTEN BY Dr. ALAN PATEMAN
ISBN: 978-1-909132-58-0
eBook ISBN: 978-1-909132-64-1

Published By:
APMI Publications
In Partnership with Truth for the Journey Books **20**
Email: publications@alanpateman.com
www.AlanPatemanMinistries.com

Acknowledgements:
Author/Design/Senior Editor/Publisher: Apostle Dr. Alan Pateman
Editing/Proofreading/Research: Dr. Jennifer Pateman
Computer Administration/Office Manager: Dr. Dorothea Struhlik
Cover Image Credit: www.PosterMyWall.com

Unless otherwise indicated, all scriptural quotations are from the HOLY BIBLE, NEW INTERNATIONAL VERSION ®. NIV ®. Copyright © 1973, 1978, 1984 by the International Bible Society. Used by permission of Zondervan Publishing House. All rights reserved.

*Where scriptures appear with special emphasis (**in bold**, italic or <u>underlined</u>) we have edited them ourselves in order to bring focused attention within the context of this subject being taught.*

❖

Dedication

I would like to dedicate this book to my good friend and colleague Apostle Doctor Benjamin Ayim Asare, for your love, partnership, dedication and business advise.

❖
Table of Contents

❖

Acknowledgements

I t is a privilege when one is studying, to be able to read the great volume of books that exist on our shelves, written by anointed men and women of God.

We don't have to look too far to find the answers or the teaching course on the particular subject that we need to enhance the role that God has given to us.

Therefore I want to acknowledge those who took time to put pen to paper!

Let us, as mere men and women who have been called of God, allow the Holy Spirit to teach us, that we would be prepared to take on the anointed task to which He has appointed us.

"God chooses, the Spirit tests, man responds."

❖

Introduction

Over the years I have been hosting leadership gatherings around the world, of which I am very grateful and honoured. However, in my travels I have been consistently challenged by the lack of understanding that prevails.

Firstly the lack of understanding of what it means to be a leader and what qualifications are necessary; secondly the lack of insight people seem to have of leadership from a New Testament point of view and the subsequent "out-working" of church "structure" i.e., leadership as seen in scripture.

It's disconcerting because as a result of this ignorance we tend to get caught up in the extremes that exist that provide no real way forward at all. So within these chapters, I want to continue from my book, "Laying Foundations" and discuss *what's next?* And what it means to be a leader. What qualifies us? And who appointed us?

Titles are also misused – certainly within the apostolic movement today. Therefore we will also discover what it means to lift one-self-up to be a bishop! As many currently perceive that the title of "bishop" exceeds that of the "apostle." We must clear up this confusion within the body of Christ.

However let it be understood from the very onset of this subject – right here in the introduction - that it is not now, nor will it ever be my intention to use this material to violate, subject, mislead, manipulate or control others, which is often wrongly "perceived" about the apostolic.

Shedding Some Light

Instead my heart towards this vast subject is to help bring much needed clarity, as there is so much out there that helps bring much "confusion-to-the-table." My intention in teaching about the Apostolic is only to shed some light on "all-things-apostolic" as they should be according to New Testament scriptures.

None of us should ever manipulate or control the work and move of the Holy Spirit or the lives of any individual committed to networking apostolically - in any capacity.

Dr. Bill Hamon in his book titled, **"Apostles, Prophets and the Coming Moves of God,"** on page 49 says, "although 'structure' is good and necessary we must never lose sight of the fact that we are ONE BODY. When structure stands in the way or when we worship or idolize our structures rather than Jesus Christ who is the HEAD of ONE BODY, then we have moved away from the Holy Spirit and truth.

Unity recognizes that there is ONE BODY. Disunity segregates and divides. We do not become members of a club or organization – we are members of the APOSTOLIC BODY of CHRIST (Ephesians 2:19-22).

We must not present ourselves in a said 'Association' or 'Network' in such a way to imply that those who do not believe and worship the same way as ourselves are out of order with God or are in some kind of error. This is not the prerogative of some kind of Pope Initiative, whether it is the Catholic, Charismatic, Pentecostal, Evangelical, Kingdom, Faith, Prophetic or the Apostolic kind.

We all need to appreciate that each person and fellowship has a responsibility to follow their own revelations, convictions and practices, but not to impose them upon the corporate body of Christ. Such presumptuous declarations, teachings and actions cause divisions in the body of Christ. Every erroneous Christian group has established certain doctrines and practices that are unique to them. This then makes them an exclusive, 'elected' group that sees itself as superior to all others" (Hamon 49).

Exclusivism Leads to Cults

He also says, "exclusivism leads to cults" that, "the manifestations of this attitude are seen in the extreme groups that arose during the time of the Holiness and Pentecostal

Movements: Mormonism, Christian Scientists and Jehovah Witnesses. But sad to say, there are also some of the extreme right that are still counted as 'mainline' Christian denominations who believe that they are the only true people of God.

They base this conviction on a certain baptism formula, way of worship, church order or some other unique doctrine or practice."

"No one man or group has it all. The New Testament scriptures emphatically and repeatedly declare that Christ has only ONE church here on planet earth. No denominational, fellowship, network, association or restoration camp makes up the entirety of the Church.

Every born again, blood washed, sanctified child of God is a member of Christ's Church. They may be Charismatic Catholics, Evangelicals, Pentecostals, Prophetic people or Present-Truth Apostolic people. We are only parts of the whole and members in particular of the corporate body of Christ.

Life is found in the Cluster

All truth and life are found in the whole, not just in one particular part or member. We need each other and will never come to maturity and fullness of truth without each other. The New Wine is in the cluster – not just in one individual grape (Isaiah 65:8)" (Hamon 49).

This however does not detract from the responsibility of any church or network from fulfilling the commission given by the Lord Jesus Christ to "go and make disciples... and teaching them..." (Matthew 28:16-20)

> *According to the grace of God which was given to me, as a wise master builder I have laid the foundation, and another builds on it. But let each one take heed how he builds on it. For no other foundation can anyone lay than that which is laid, which is Jesus Christ.*
> (1 Corinthians 3:10, 11 NKJV)

**"The great need of the day is growth,
balance and maturity in Sonship."**

❖

CHAPTER 1

Relationship between the Apostolic and the Local Church

L et's look at the relationship that should exist between the apostle and the local church - how they should relate. We will look at how the authoritative structure within the church works. Also we will look at gifts - for example is an apostle a position of **"office" or "gift?"** This we can answer straight away.

First the Apostle

First the apostle was given as a gift, as seen in Ephesians 4:11ff; 1 Corinthians 12:28. God has appointed ministry gifts in the church and this guarantees that they *(the church)* will function properly.

Ulf Ekman explains it like this: "When the bible says that God has appointed 'first apostles,' it does not mean that He has placed them up on a pedestal. Instead, it means that the apostle has been placed *at the very front.*

The idea of a vertical triangle with some sort of pope seated at the top should be discarded. Imagine instead a horizontal triangle that looks like a plow. God has positioned the apostle at the tip of this plow. The apostle can be likened to a *general practitioner.* He has the ability to operate in all of the ministry offices" (Ekman 35).

"Apostle and prophet teams then set pastors and pastoral elders over the churches to guard, feed and lead the flock of believers like a shepherd *(Acts 15:32; 16:4,18,25; 2 Corinthians 1:19; 2 Thessalonians 1:1; Acts 20:28)*" (Hamon 53).

In other words the apostle has a governing office and can function in any of the gifts. Therefore the apostle has an **office to govern,** along with ministry gifts and the authority to establish.

Sent or Stayed

Not all apostles travel, some are senior pastors of apostolic churches; apostle James is an example, he was considered an apostle in scripture, he did not actually leave the church in Jerusalem. Seemingly, he never ministered outside of Jerusalem. But apostle Paul travelled continually during his thirty-plus years of ministry.

His longest stay at any local church was two years in Ephesus. So this begs the question; **"can an apostle be a**

'sent-one' and be a 'stayed-one' at the same time?" Yes! So long as he is *establishing, building* and *fulfilling* a mandate that he has ultimately been sent by God to fulfil.

However this depends largely on his "gifting" too and not just his "office." Now his *office* is one thing, and his *gifting* helps him to carry out the mandate upon his *office.* For example, an apostle whose main gifting is to be a pastor is able to *build* right where he is. He is able to have an international mind-set *(not parochial in his vision)* and possess the spiritual capacity to travel and be "sent" but also has the capacity to "stay."

Now in addition to this, it must be stated that all the gifts are EQUAL - they just have different tasks to do. Likewise all the "offices" are *equal;* they just operate with different gifting. For example a local elder who has a governing-office to "oversee," is one who has been given dominion in a certain area.

The Great Connector

However when it comes to the local church in relation to the apostle - it has to be said that being part of one body - includes being **"connected"** with the rest of the body. And a great part of what the apostle does is through "connections." **He is a great connector.** The Holy Spirit uses the apostolic ministry more than any other to do His great global networking!

Now having said all this - any position of authority or given office of governing authority *(whether apostle, elder/ bishop)* is not dictatorial but submissive - particularly the apostle who is able to "recognise" what God has already established and continues to establish.

It is also crucial to observe here that once the local elders have been set in and their role established - it is THEY who have the authority over the local church and *not* the apostle. Now of course he still has authority to bring correction like a shepherd-father-figure would - but he does not stay around to carry this out. His role is to oversee.

To view this in scripture we go to the verses quoted below in order to highlight or showcase this point perfectly - when Paul was troubled to write with much concern to warn the church in Corinth of his pending rebuke!

> *I'm afraid that I may come and find you different from what I want you to be, and that you may find me different from what you want me to be...*
>
> *I already warned you when I was with you the second time, and even though I'm not there now, I'm warning you again. When I visit you again, I won't spare you. That goes for all those who formerly led sinful lives as well as for all the others. Since you want proof that Christ is speaking through me, that's what you'll get. Christ isn't weak in dealing with you. Instead, he makes his power felt among you. He was weak when he was crucified, but by God's power he lives.*
>
> *(2 Corinthians 12:20; 13:3-4 GW)*

Obviously the apostle has a continuing position of responsibility when it comes to the local church but he is not there to stay and to run the local church or implement the local vision! This again is the role of the set leading elders.

Let us move on now to the next step and take a look at how apostolic teams in particular should function and work together. Before we do this let me point out ever so briefly how important structure is. The spine or backbone is our natural structure. None of us can live without it! And spiritually speaking the same is true also. Even Satan's kingdom has structure to it.

We see this show-cased in the sixth chapter of the book of Ephesians and verse 12 where it says; "This is not a wrestling match against a human opponent. We are wrestling with rulers, authorities, the powers who govern this world of darkness, and spiritual forces that control evil in the heavenly world" *(GW)*. It is very distinct here that there are varying levels in the kingdom of darkness, levels of authority or hierarchy to execute its mandates.

Kingdom has Structure

This represents none other than a governing "structure," yet perhaps in reverse from that of the kingdom of God. And by saying, **in reverse** I don't suggest for a moment that this means *equal-to* God's kingdom, by no means! Yet Satan once knew just how the kingdom of God functioned and was internally structured... therefore he most certainly would have modelled his best attempts at organizing his hordes of darkness - upon what he saw working with pristine order and condition within the kingdom of God!

Structure is valued by those who understand how it works and by structure I don't mean that we get all wrapped up in knots because we have adopted some form of legalism. Nevertheless "structure-less-ness" is far from freedom - but more like anarchy and chaos and who can have success in the midst of confusion?

Anyhow take business for example; they could never thrive without structure. Organizations would collapse the world over without structure and so would every great building of antiquity that we know! From the tower of London and Big Ben to the Eiffel tower - still known as the tallest structure in Paris! Nothing of significance can remain standing without some form of structure holding it up!

So **we must not be "structure-shy" especially within the church** where we tend to feel obliged to run a "free-for-all" and expect it to work! **It must not be said by our enemies that the body of Christ has no backbone or that we are spineless!** But nor let us try and create our own image of structure based upon what we think church should be like… No! Rather we should submit ourselves to what God has already laid out in scripture to work irrespective and notwithstanding our misguided reservations towards… the apostolic ministry!

Void of Spiritual Backbone!

Instead we should shout, "Welcome back!" For the church as we know it - has indeed been feeble and without strength - yes even much of it has been guilty of being spineless and void of spiritual backbone! But now is the time to embrace true spiritual structure as Christ deemed fit to bestow upon the church and to recognize once again the importance of this "apostolic ministry" within His body. Who are we to resist? We must work-with and not against true spiritual structure.

It is true to say that it has never been enough for the spiritually immature - "floppy-n-floaty" *(freshly filled with new wine Christians)* to get this great and awesome job done! Nor has it ever been enough just for the "stuffy-n-religious-bookworm-types" to give their official nod to everything! What we need is the precious working of God's Holy Spirit, the power of His Word and the coming together of His mighty body worldwide - "a-great-working-together" - to get this great and divine commission complete!

So as we continue then, from our brief look at the supposed "hierarchy" of Satan's kingdom - let's us now look at the "structure-of-authority" as it should exist within God's kingdom - according to scripture *(in other words apostolic teams working together)* - as follows:

1). Main forces of human leadership:

A] Apostolic teams and presbyteries *(elders)*

1. Both usually PLURAL
2. A shepherd is a pastor
   a) Shepherd *(singular)* always refers to Jesus *(Acts 20:17)*
   b) Elders *(plural)* are overseers *(or bishops)* or shepherds *(see also 1 Peter 5:1-2)*
3. As shepherds *(elders)* are united, so will their flocks be

B] Elder's responsibility is to govern - conservation *(1 Timothy 5:17; Titus 1:5)*

    a) In the OT the elder's place was at the gate

    b) Their function: judgement, counsel and government

    c) The NT concurs with this

C] Apostolic team's function is extensive *(Romans 15:20-21)*

    a) Reach the unreached

    b) They did not operate alone

D] Governing body in an area is sovereign

    a) Same applies to a family, mother and father are sovereign

    Independence and sovereignty are not the same

    b) Sovereign: accountable to God

    c) Independent: out from under God's authority possibly?

E] Apostolic teams

    Mobile

    Top authority of church extension

    Presbyteries

    Local/resident

    Govern locally conservation

    a) Balance is 50% emphasis on either side in NT church

      b) The current balance is 98% conservation and 2% extension

F] **There is** *no place for independence* **in Christianity**

2). Interdependence:

A] Apostles appoint elders *(Acts 14:21-23)*

      a) After elders become installed, a group of believers becomes a church

B] Apostles sent out by elders *(Acts 13:1-4)*

      a) They became apostles after being prayed for and sent out *(Acts 14:14)*

      b) They were selected by the Holy Spirit from the most experienced and fruitful

      c) Then new leadership emerges from the less experienced

C] Reproductive cycle *(Acts 16:1; 1 Thessalonians 2:6)*

      a) Apostle means: one sent forth

      b) It all starts with God the Father

3). Jesus set the pattern:

A] The first Apostle *(Hebrew 3:1)*

      a) Women have a place *(Luke 8:1-3)*

B] The Early Church was mobile

C] Apostolic attestation

      a) It takes the supernatural to make Gentiles obedient *(Romans 15:18-19)*

      b) *(2 Corinthians 12:12)*

D] Marks of the apostle

    a) Perseverance, character, not giving up

    b) Signs, wonders and mighty deeds

E] The issue is NOT apostle succession, but apostolic ministry (*1 Corinthians 4:20*)

❖

CHAPTER 2

Establishing Leadership

It is my desire in this chapter to help people understand whether they are *called or appointed* by God, to whatever position or realm He has decided. We are not looking here to discover the depths of how a ministry operates in its function, but simply how to be prepared in the positioning of ourselves within the body of Christ. Only then will those in authority be able to recognize that which God has imparted within us; which in turn *releases* us into our destiny.

The democratic society we live in is far removed from the definition of a kingdom, where a king rules because he inherited the throne! Democracy differs in that her leaders are elected and not inherited. A system where leadership roles are open to the talented and asserted, but as for the kingdom of God, it operates on an entirely different premise.

...I warn everyone among you not to estimate and think of himself more highly than he ought [not to have an exaggerated opinion of his own importance], but *to rate his ability with sober judgment,* each according to the degree of faith apportioned by God to him.

(Romans 12:3 AMP)

Jesus Himself appointed offices of service, found in Ephesians 4:11, only Jesus Himself through the Holy Spirit gives this authority to men. **When we assume authority rather than receive authority we are on dangerous ground.** Self-exaltation is the promotion of self-purposes rather than seeking first the kingdom of God. Consider those who have been called but not yet appointed, who then commission themselves and who end up serving themselves; our commission can only come from the Lord.

Chosen from among Men

Spiritual leaders are **"...chosen from among men"** and are "...**appointed** to act on behalf of men in things relating to God." Furthermore, **"one does not appropriate for himself the honour... but he is called by God..."** Just as Jesus, "...did not exalt Himself...but was **appointed**..." *(Hebrews 5:1, 4, 5 AMP)*

Appointment comes from God alone, even Jesus did not assume His place, but was appointed by the Father. We may be called, but we also require appointment. Consider Paul who in Romans 1:1 in the NIV states that he was both *"called"* and *"separated."*

The call comes first then the appointment! You may have been called before the earth began or while you were still in the womb but that was not when you stepped into your **"office!"** You step into your call *[salvation]* before you ever step into your office.

Testing of Years

Note: Paul went through years of testing once he submitted himself to the leaders at Antioch. *"They must first be tested; and then... let them serve..." (1 Timothy 3:10)*

Separated actually means chosen, Jesus said *"Many are called, but few are chosen..." (Matthew 22:14)* **Meaning that not many make it through those *testing* periods**, but the few who make it are those who have been successfully *separated* unto the Lord! All ministries must go through a period of testing and preparation *(this preparation varies from gift to gift)* before we go through or move through into our assigned assignment, our appointed time!

There are *offices* and *positions of service,* mentioned in the bible, *(1 Corinthians 12:28)* **"And God has appointed** these in the church: first apostles, second prophets, third teachers, after that ... helps..." *(NKJV)* Paul during those first years in Antioch did not occupy a five fold office *(Ephesians 4:11)* **in fact he served in the ministry of helps, then was promoted to the office of a teacher (2 Timothy 1:11; Acts 13:1).**

John Bevere says in his book **"Thus Saith the Lord,"** "Not only would Paul be tested in the realm of helps but in the office of teacher as well. When Paul was promoted from teacher to apostle we again see how God chooses and separates those that He wants to fill certain offices or positions" (Bevere 120).

In Acts 13:1-2 we can see how Paul is listed along with other teachers in Antioch and how the Holy Spirit wanted them to be separated unto Him. The appointed time had finally come, the one who had been called to be an apostle all those years earlier on the road to Damascus in Acts 9:15 had finally, after many years of testing and loyal service, now been separated unto God to be an apostle.

First he was *called* then he served in *helps,* later in the *office of a teacher* and then lastly in that of an *apostle.* Why? Because Paul was faithful to promote the Lord and not himself *(1 Corinthians 4:2).*

Note: God used the established leadership whom Paul had faithfully served...

> *Then, having fasted and prayed, and laid hands on them,* **THEY SENT THEM** *away. So, being sent out by the Holy Spirit, they went...*
>
> *(Acts 13:3-4 NKJV)*

God did not use anyone Paul was not already in submission to; instead he used an established authority that had already been set up in Antioch. **God will not undermine the leadership in the body of Christ in order to raise someone up into a position of leadership. Why, because your character is far more important than your *gifting.***

❖

CHAPTER 3

Discernment of Gifting

Let us continue and move on and look at the concept of **"gift discernment."** Exactly what has God graced our lives with? Just like Paul, we must be able to "recognise" who we are in Christ and what we have been called to "do," without this, it is inevitable that we will both be "unfruitful" and "ineffective" *(regardless of any good intentions!)*

Therefore we must discover what God's plan for our individual lives really is and more importantly what His plan is to benefit other people's lives through ours. Gifting is "always" for others and not for self! So along with the gift we must also recognise who is going to "benefit" and what exactly is He looking to "influence" with His kingdom. God always has a strategy plan!

*Before I formed you in the womb I knew you, before you were born **I set you apart; I appointed you** as a prophet to the nations.*

(Jeremiah 1:5)

Evidently it becomes a major necessity for us to have clarity on this issue. We must begin by accepting the fact that "divine distinction" does exist and that we must work together with it not against it. Quite simply, there are many folks today who are failing to see this "divine distinction" not only in their own lives but also in the lives of others.

As a result many are "struggling" and "straining" themselves to be something that God has not called them to be. We often succumb to the peer pressure of becoming what others perceive for us rather than what God has "appointed" for us.

Today it would be true to say that there exists so much confusion between **"body gifting"** and **"ministry calling,"** something that has caused pain, heartache and much "disillusionment."

To help clear this up let's look at four major factors that need to be considered when it comes to ministry gifting.

The Sense of Call

Today I believe that we often mix up "desire" with "call." Of course, the scripture tells us to desire the best gifts *(see 1 Corinthians 12:31)*. However desire can never override call. First and foremost any desires must line up with the will of God for our lives.

The Desire for the Work

The call always comes first from God's point of view as we see here in Jeremiah 1:5; "Before you were formed in the womb I called you" *(appointed, sanctified, set apart, separated, consecrated and dedicated)*. However this was news to Jeremiah. Who was less than ecstatic about the proposal. Rather he went into an immediate verbal inventory of all the excuses and reasons why the opposite was in fact true. Not unlike the rest of us do!

Inadequacy often rears its ugly head in the face of stepping up to the call. Nevertheless in the midst of trauma we can discover the "desire" to serve the Lord.

With all this in mind we need to distinguish what desire in this context actually means. It goes beyond just a human sense of looking to enjoy something. Rather in this context it is more of an "inner yearning," a "knowing" that we must face this call or we are going to die! *(It can feel this intense; like your whole life depends on it, even before you really understand why)*.

And while it might be possible to enjoy serving God, desire from the inner man is something quite different; that inward yearning we spoke of, goes much deeper; according to the Strong's it is akin to "jealousy" or being "zealous" *(see Strong's #G2206)*.

Exercise the Gift

A man's ministry makes room for itself. A genuine call from God will manifest itself - if it is exercised properly.

God does not appoint us to a position of "spiritual inertia" *(inactivity, lethargy, disinterest, inaction or unwillingness)*. Rather He appoints and anoints for ACTION *(faith without works is dead!)* So there is a built-in dynamic to this "call" of God that we all face and it only finds *expression* through continual practice and not "theory!"

Fruitfulness, a Sign of Ministry

So many people lay claim to ministries in advance of "fruitfulness" and "appointment," when in fact fruitfulness is the real sign of ministry. **"Do not neglect your gift**, which was given you through a prophetic message when the body of elders laid their hands on you" *(1 Timothy 4:14)*; "…**fan into flame the gift** of God," *(2 Timothy 1:6)*; "Each one should **use whatever gift** he has received to serve others, faithfully administering God's grace in its various forms" *(1 Peter 4:10)*.

There is a distinction in kind, between a talent, which we were born with and a gift imparted by the Holy Spirit. It is noticeable in Paul's ministry that he was not averse to using his natural talents in his service for the Lord. For example he was obviously intellectually gifted but also practically so and at times used his natural abilities to support his own ministry *(see Acts 18:3 for tent making)*.

But it is also important to see how Paul laid such talents aside when it came to operating in revelation *(see 1 Corinthians 2:1-3)*. God uses both in the leader but in fact, it is dedication of all that we have and are, which removes the clear distinction between natural talent and divine gift in the leader.

Every Called Person has a Handicap

The great heroes of the bible had handicaps even those with mighty signs and wonders; they were mere humans with many limitations and flaws. Moses committed murder and had a terrible speech impediment. Miriam fuelled a conspiracy against Moses during the wilderness journey of the Israelites. David committed adultery and murder. A harmless little old lady intimidated Elijah. And when the chips were down, Peter denied even knowing Jesus! Saul of Tarsus rounded up Christians and threw them in jail or had them stoned and it goes on.

I like the fact that none of these heroes were larger than life on their own. It gives us hope, because most of us were anything but a success before we met the Lord. If anything, God specialises in taking people who are self-willed, arrogant, or just plain ordinary and making a success of them. By successful, I don't mean rich and famous, but humble, loving, and generous and becoming the best they can be in Christ.

What seems to be our tragedy becomes our triumph. We learn how to turn the "messes" of our lives into "messages" and how to change the "tests" into "testimonies," and as my wife often says, "turn our cares into prayers; our worry into worship and last but not least how to find peace in the pain." Our strength is always in God.

What is our biggest hindrance to success - is it failure? - No! We are our own hindrance! Making mistakes is not a hindrance for victory! We see in scripture when Elijah went straight from a great victory into a great flop! Jonah, everything God told him to do - he did the exact opposite! We have all come to that place where we have found our problems were not really the issue; instead we discovered that our problems were actually God given opportunities!

This transpires simply because problems can help make us people who reach out past and beyond our natural abilities. Whereas a person who reaches out to God without any problems or challenges whatsoever, sees little if any change, growth or increase etc.

Problems represent NEEDS!

In reality who needs to look for problems? Problems exist and God has called every one of us to be problem solvers. **Problems represent NEEDS!** Problems are not wrong. They are not negatives if we look at them positively.

They are needs that God has called us and given us the ability and anointing to meet and solve. For sake of illustration there were two salesmen who came back from Africa, one was down and the other was up - thrilled to bits. One said, *"They don't wear shoes in Africa - it's hopeless."* The other said, *"No one has shoes in Africa, they all need our shoes!"*

God told us that we are to get a harvest, to multiply and reproduce. That means we must see and experience "increase" because **God has said. In other words, blessing is not a feeling but a condition** therefore it is important to consider this vital fact:

God's expression for our lives is an expression of His promises.

❖

CHAPTER 4

Spiritual Gifts vs. Governing Authority

It is true to say, that being "gifted" does not automatically make you "autonomous" *(independent)*. In other words, none of us are an end in ourselves nor can we have authority in ourselves! None of us can function independently from the rest of the "body" and thrive or survive!

In actual fact our gift only operates and functions in its fullest degree and glory when it is functioning with the rest of the body and submitted-to-the-correct-authorities within the body.

Has the Lord indeed spoken only by Moses? Has He not spoken also by us?

(Numbers 12:2 AMP)

There is some confusion at large in the body of Christ today, over this very issue, because immaturity and misunderstanding say that because a person operates in a "gifting" *(albeit genuine)* this automatically gives him or her governing-authority. Absolutely Not!

Spiritual Gifting vs. Governing Office

Let's look at it like this: it is a grave mistake to confuse mere spiritual gifting with governing-office. All of us as believers have a measure of authority but this amounts to the general believer's authority and does not include governing-authority or being in an office of authority within the body of Christ.

Therefore having a gift does not give anyone of us an automatic position-of-authority, just a general authority, which is the right of "every" believer. In fact we all have been given significant-authority in order to lay hands on the sick and to raise the dead!

Along with general authority as a believer we have general gifts that have been distributed amongst us - but none of this gives us an automatic "office-of-authority." To help explain this further, scripture tells us clearly that it is the Holy Spirit who is the giver of the gifts but that Jesus Himself is the One who places certain individuals into positions of governing-authority *(called offices)*.

An ordinary believer's authority is something we can gain overnight! But to have a governing-authority in the body of Christ is something else altogether. Irreparable damage has been done because of the lack of adequate understanding in this very area *(see 1 Corinthians 12:4-31; Ephesians 4:11-12).*

If a person begins to operate in a legitimate gift but after some time refuses to yield themselves over to an established authority structure, then that gifting will become distorted and perverted; warped and void of purity because of its false agenda. **It's far too easy for a person to become disillusioned when they have no real accountability.** Distortion develops with misuse and lack of submission to God's governing authorities.

Now but Not Automatic

The same person, who is gifted now, is not automatically ready to have governing-authority NOW! Mere gifting never gave any man governing-authority, **this only comes via divine appointment and preparation**; being made ready through testing and faithful serving!

For illustration purposes let us refer to Miriam and Aaron who spoke against Moses in the bible *(Numbers 12:1-2).* Whether they did this openly or privately is not made clear but nonetheless God heard their conversation and was not too happy about it.

We must consider that although both Aaron and Miriam were genuinely gifted and already had some position-of-authority, it was Moses nonetheless who was God's "governing-authority" at that time. Their supernatural gifting *(whether legitimate or not)* afforded neither of them any room whatsoever to usurp Moses governmental-office.

This was a direct insult to God. So serious in fact was this offence before God that Miriam became leprous because of it *(Number 12:10).* However both were forgiven and restored, nevertheless it reveals the dangers of *usurping* God-given and appointed authority. It illustrates perfectly the difference between mere *spiritual gifting* and *governing-authority.*

It might be true to say that not all false prophets *set out* to be false, rather they *become* that way. Just like Miriam and Aaron would have become false, if they had continued using their "gifting" to try and *out-rank* their brother *(Moses).*

It must be understood therefore that no man or woman can assume the kind of authority that Moses had been given by God - certainly not on the grounds of spiritual-gifting! God alone appoints individuals to such positions and we can see just how vehemently God defends it!

We must never forget that none of us can successfully operate outside of God's authority-structure, as our human ability to remain authentic, trustworthy, faithful, reliable, genuine, dependable or accurate - outside of His boundaries of authority - is zero! In fact to remain true rather than false within our gift capacity, we must remain continuously submitted to God given, ordained and appointed authority. No human reasoning or logic can add anything to or take away from this concept.

Conclusion:

In short, we must learn *not* to hold our own opinions too highly or be threatened by the credentials of others. We must work hard to show ourselves approved and be diligent to get genuine instruction and guidance from the Holy Spirit; who will never lead us to usurp authority.

For our gifts to flourish and to live peaceful lives we must not violate the boundaries of God's authoritative structure and governing authority.

We can only enjoy the true benefits of authority, whilst we cooperate with it!

❖

CHAPTER 5

Authority - Who has it?

We all know that we have been given authority through Jesus Christ, to overcome in this life, to lay hands on the sick and to cast out demons etc. Spiritually speaking this means we reign in life and have dominion.

Nevertheless we are all part of the body of Christ, which has a specific structure with leadership - called Church. Whether we perceive we are individually gifted or not - this gives no automatic-right for any of us to become a leader within the local church. *(Qualification for leadership - authoritative office if God appoints - takes a number of years).*

Given to me was all authority in heaven and on earth.
(Matthew 28:18 YLT)

However within this chapter I would like to begin by speaking about the apostolic, the apostles in general. Which means this chapter is not a written spotlight based upon the believer's authority but more specifically in regard to the five-fold-governmental-authority.

(Note: successive chapters will touch on elders and deacons including whether the title "bishop" is just another word for "elder" currently mistaken as the "supreme-title" of the church, replacing that of the apostle!)

Who has Authority?

First and foremost, authority begins and ends with Christ but the question is; who else has authority?

To help answer this we are going to look at the five fold ministry gifts, ordained by none other than Christ Himself and known as the **"resurrection apostles."** The one that we will focus on the most in this chapter is the apostle but before we continue let me make this statement,

"Authority and responsibility can only be given by those who have it."

Our opening scripture above (Matthew 28:18) reveals very clearly that ALL authority - both in heaven and on the earth belongs to Christ. That is a lot of authority! And it's not a power sharing scheme either... all means all. Jesus will never **SHARE** authority power with anyone, but He does **GIVE** it to those He delegates *(chief components in this of course are the ascension or five fold ministry gifts).*

Let's see this again briefly in the following verses: "All authority in heaven and on earth has been given to me" *(Matthew 28:18)*. "It was **he who gave some to be apostles, some to be prophets, some to be evangelists, and some to be pastors and teachers**, to prepare God's people for works of service, so that the body of Christ may be built up" *(Ephesians 4:11-12)*.

"Ministry Gifts" then, exist primarily for the building up and preparing of God's people for works of service. It could be said like this: principally they have earthly authority and receive their ordination directly from the Lord Himself, without human involvement. Such was the case with the original disciples who lived with Jesus during His earthly ministry.

Equally so, however, was the case with Paul who was "...one born out of due time..." *(1 Corinthians 15:8 KJV)* "The things that mark an apostle - signs, wonders and miracles - were done among you with great perseverance" *(2 Corinthians 12:12)*.

Ultimate Authority

Therefore it is true to say that the original New Testament apostles literally had "ultimate authority" on this earth, which was no small thing! For instance if there was a dispute regarding doctrine, then the apostles were the final adjudicators; they had the last say.

Some of the apostles by their very nature also fulfilled the **offices of elder** *(bishop)* **and overseer.** The reverse however does not necessarily apply. A person recognised as an elder is not automatically an apostle or other ministry gift to the church. The apostle is perhaps the most difficult of the five ministry gifts to explain.

Known to us then in more familiar terms as the "five fold ministries" these are perhaps better called the "five ascension gifts" as we already saw revealed in Ephesians 4:11 above: **"apostle, prophet, evangelist, pastor and teacher."**

Let me point out however, these are not just gifts of the Holy Spirit per se, they are "office and gifting" combined, an extension of Christ's headship ministry to the church. **Their primary ministry and function is to teach, train, activate and mature the saints for works of service** *(Ephesians 4:12-13)*.

Laying Foundations

As one of the five and concerning the apostle in particular - the apostle is a **"foundation-laying"** ministry *(Ephesians 2:20)* that we see in the New Testament, establishing new churches *(i.e. Paul's missionary journeys)*, correcting error by establishing proper order and structure *(first epistle to the Corinthians)*, and acting as an oversight ministry that fathers other ministries *(see 1 Corinthians 4:15; 2 Corinthians 11:28)*.

The New Testament apostle has a **"revelatory-anointing"** *(Ephesians 3:5)*. Some major characteristics are great patience and manifestations of signs, wonders and miracles. However we will know more and see greater manifestations surrounding the ministry of the "apostle" during the peak of the Apostolic Movement to come.

A keynote to point out here of course is that no person ever went or ever will walk straight into an apostolic ministry! There is always a process just as we saw with Paul: "In the church at Antioch there were prophets and teachers: Barnabas, Simeon called Niger, Lucius of Cyrene, Manaen *(who had been brought up with Herod tetrarch)* and Saul" *(Acts 13:1).* Evidently Paul was recognised operating in other ministry gifting *(teacher)* before he was commissioned by the Holy Spirit and then "sent-out" as an apostle by *(his)* the leaders.

This is a good point to remember. In other words, no one is born an apostle. It takes serious preparation and maturity to walk in that office plus it is not chosen by the individual - rather it is bestowed upon them, at God's bidding - not their own. Paul was no volunteer! God had to throw him down off his high horse first and that was just to get his attention. Rather Jesus "informed" Paul of his selection; he was not consulted!

It is a sovereign act of God. Entirely for His choosing and while many are called - few are chosen; few can walk in such an office. Therefore self-assigned or self-appointed apostles are real glutens for punishment, as scripture clearly reveals that it is no walk in the park to be a genuine apostle! It's not a title for glory, it's an office of government; spiritually weighty and generally unpopular!

The Pioneers of the Church

As spearheads and pioneers, they take the brunt of onslaught, while at the same time they faithfully lead others to victory! Not everyone has what it takes! Remembering that part of the calibre and proof of leadership is generally that other people naturally follow! It's self-explanatory, that if no one is *following*, those claiming to be in leadership status are clearly just in wishful thinking! The gift will speak for itself.

Generally if an apostle walks in a room, his presence fills the room and is felt by everyone! They possess such weight in the spirit that rarely goes unnoticed. They become recognised quickly as well as targeted and spoken about quickly! *(A lot!)* These are the true joys of apostle-hood *(with its inherent and unrelenting passion)*. No one in their right mind would sign up for a role like this; rather the Lord Himself confers it on man simply because there are no volunteers!

However to continue, the apostle will usually have one or more of the other five fold ministry gifts - as his major gifting as well; this is called his "gift-mixture." For example apostle Paul was a *teacher*. Apostle Peter was a *pastor*. Apostle Barnabas was a *prophet*. We need to look at scripture to see what kind of men these were and what they did to discover their ministries as true apostles of Christ.

The most prominent is shown in the listing found here:

Now you are the body of Christ, and each one of you is a part of it. And in the church God has appointed first of all apostles, second prophets, third teachers, then workers of miracles, also those having gifts of healing, those able to help others, those with gifts of administration, and those speaking in different kinds of tongues.

(1 Corinthians 12:27-28)

So does this apostolic ministry merely exist to bless or to build? To bless is one thing, to build is quite another. We could say it like this: to bless and just excite people all the time, requires humanism, stamina and lots of charisma! This usually results in human appreciation, generally large love-gifts and popular return bookings *(invited back!)*

Yet for God this will *never* be enough! A true apostle cannot be bought or sold. He is not a crowd pleaser. Even if he does please the crowd, that's not his primary intention.

Why? Because Jesus is not interested in *exciting crowds* but in building His church. However building with the "**Master Builder**" *(Jesus)* is genuinely **hard work!** It takes dedication on an unprecedented scale and life-long commitment *(the apostolic ministry is not for the faint hearted!)*

We can say it like this: all apostles are in it for the long haul. They don't need convincing. They don't even sprint! Rather they plod, even when everyone else is having a spiritual sugar rush; running here and there on nervous human energy! In fact by the time others collapse from weariness, the apostle just keeps on keeping on, steady and undeterred. Mature with lengthy staying power - because he has had to learn to suffer-LONG!

No Time to Waste

Apostles generally show no interest for time wasting activities and are notoriously stable. They bring order and Godly discipline wherever they go and exude an admirable stature. People are drawn to them, for all sorts of reasons, both good and bad. In other words they can attract trouble like bees to honey, or moth to a flame simply because they have been dispatched as **God's voice in the earth**; anything and everything wants to shut them up!

In order to build a master plan is required and the master designer is not haphazard. The builders need insight into God's plan and strategy for the church. The apostle in close collaboration with his prophetic teammates **seeks always to build according to the patterns shown on the "mountain" of revelation.**

> *They serve at a sanctuary that is a copy and shadow of what is in heaven. This is why Moses was warned when he was about to build the tabernacle: "See to it that you make everything according to the pattern shown you on the mountain."*
>
> (Hebrews 8:5)

Accumulated Rubbish

As it was in Nehemiah's day, there must be a clearing-away of accumulated *rubbish!* Today there exists, to a very large extent, wrong thinking in regards to the actual role of the local church. Many see it as a place to attend only when needing a *blessing.* A cavalier easy-come-easy-go attitude prevails.

In addition there are such individuals who perceive that they can justifiably manipulate the church in order to serve their own ends *(personal gain - financial, sexual or otherwise)* or simply fill a vast ego! Either way Christ is not usually front-and-centre in those types of churches!

Then there are those churches who try to embody new ideas and structures within their services and mingle it in with the old-way. Generally this effects no real or worthwhile change, but instead **introduces competition into their churches - where the old now has to compete with the new!**

We see this featured in Mark 2:21-22, "No one sews a patch of un-shrunk cloth on an old garment. If he does, the new piece will pull away from the old, making the tear worse. And no one pours new wine into old wineskins. If he does, the wine will burst the skins, and both the wine and the wineskins will be ruined. No, he pours new wine into new wineskins" *(Mark 2:21-22).*

With all intents and purposes an apostle is a prolific builder and will always have that desire to BUILD. He will establish new churches and or re-establish existing ones, but his ministry will always be the same. In fact restoration and pioneering go hand in hand for the apostle - "building" or "re-building" are the same to him - it's all building and precisely what he will be found doing. It is his calling card. To bring into order **"...to build and to establish"** *(see Jeremiah 1:10; 18:9; 31:28; 33:2).*

Unity Expressed in Diversity

Philip Mohabir in his book, **"Hands of Jesus"** says that, "Paul sets forth in Ephesians 4 the core values and essential virtues that form the kernel from which local church life and practice flow. They are unity expressed in diversity, maturity, stability and corporeity. The ascended Lord gave apostles, prophets, evangelists, pastors and teachers to the church to build these characteristics in the very fiber of local church life.

He has given five gifts for this purpose. We cannot do it with three or even four. In His infinite wisdom, He knew we need five. God is generous but not superfluous. Any other structure, system, strategy, or man-made method will fail to produce the kind of church that Jesus wants and for which He died.

But now is the time when the Lord is restoring the apostolic and apostles to the church. Now is the time for the whole body of Christ to experience the authority and anointing of apostles just as it was in the book of Acts. To see the church rise to its full potential and built according to New Testament pattern, we must rise in vision and faith. To see the church become all that the Lamb died to make it, **we need another apostolic reformation.**

In these days the Lord is preparing the church, His Bride, for glory, equipping her to reap a final gigantic harvest and at the same time preparing the world for judgment.

Worldwide Penetration

As Dr. Sam Matthews said, let us allow the Holy Spirit to orchestrate us into a worldwide penetration of the gospel. **It is time to become part of the second apostolic reformation.** As mentioned before 'the vision is rushing to completion.'

The five ascension gifts are not optional extras, but essential imperatives, ordained by God for the church. Their importance and role to the body are a divine arrangement by Father, Son and Holy Spirit. We cannot fulfil the apostolic mission of the church without their active presence. If the church 2000 years ago needed them, how much more do we need them today when the days are so much more evil? Oh, how we need them!" (Mohabir 24, 28-29)

❖

CHAPTER 6

Who Ordains Who?

Ordination is a biblical principle and directive that is found throughout both the Old and New Testaments. It can be seen in operation first of all in the Garden of Eden and then repeatedly during every spiritual awakening right through to the Acts of the Apostles and the early church. There is however, reference to ordination before this time by the prophet Ezekiel, where he says of Lucifer:

You were anointed as a guardian cherub, for so I ordained you. You were on the holy mount of God; you walked among the fiery stones.

(Ezekiel 28:14)

He prophesies concerning Satan that, prior to his rebellion and fall, he was ordained *(or set in place)* by God as an anointed cherub on the holy mount of God.

This pre-time prophetic revelation serves to show the importance of ordination within the kingdom and body of the Lord Jesus Christ. His rejection due to pride, led to rebellion, violence and disorder.

...God is not a God of disorder...

(1 Corinthians 14:33)

Ordaining is God's Nature

The importance and reason for **ordaining ministers is fundamental** to the nature and character of God. He loves order - He created it and used it to bring to birth the world and everything in it - including mankind. He ordained light and darkness. He ordained earth and sky, land and sea and in so doing provided a structured environment for mankind.

Now the Lord God had planted a garden in the East, in Eden; and there he put the man he had formed.

(Genesis 2:8)

When God put Adam in the Garden of Eden, the **wording used implies appointment or ordination**. Adam was firstly appointed to a position provided and prepared for him, later on in verse 15. God completes the call by defining his responsibility i.e. to *"work it"* *(the garden)* and take care of it.

The principle itself is that of one who has authority, *delegating to another a commission of responsibility and therefore a realm of spiritual authority.* It is the highest form of *"service"* within the body of Christ. Jesus said, *"He who would be chief among you, would be the servant of all!"*

There are different degrees of ordination as there are different measures of service.

Ordination therefore can be defined thus:

- The appointment of an individual to a place or position of authority

- The delegation to an individual of an area of responsibility. Moses ordained elders to assist in the management of the mighty nation of Israel *(Exodus 18:25)*

- He also ordained the priesthood, with Aaron as high priest *(Exodus 28:1)*

- Towards the end of his life and ministry he ordained Joshua - his disciple - to be his successor

Moses did as the Lord commanded him. He took Joshua and made him stand before Eleazar the priest and the whole assembly. Then he laid his hands on him and commissioned him, as the Lord instructed through Moses *(Numbers 27:18-23).*

The Pattern Continues

Samuel and David, Elijah and Elisha and many others, each exemplifying ordination as God's purpose for their day. Then Jesus speaking to His disciple's states quite clearly that He chose and ordained them to go and bear fruit *(John 15:16).*

When speaking to Peter after His resurrection, He commissions Peter to feed and take care of his sheep. In every instance mentioned, each individual had laid aside their own will and desire to take up and submit to, the will and desire of God. In so doing, they fulfilled their destiny and call, to powerful effect!

Who Ordains Who?

Over the years, many have come to me and asked that I would ordain them. Usually I have mixed emotions regarding their request, as not all are genuine in their quest to be ordained. Motives are very important. Before I give any answer, whether it being "Yes or No," **I first ask a number of questions.**

The following are an example:

Am I their apostle? Who have these individuals submitted to so far? And have they already an apostle whom they are in relationship with? *(As you do not want to usurp another's authority and build on another's foundation...)*

Have they split from somebody else, therefore creating a church split? If so, that would have to be dealt with as this will cause them problems later on and reflect on the Lord!

Are they looking to be in association or affiliation? *(There is a big difference between the two.)* The first is that they may take the relationship lightly. In the second case, you are their apostle i.e. Father in the faith... All this has to be qualified for future relationship development; remembering that every relationship must have a foundation of understanding which gives clear boundaries to both parties; stopping any confusion or misgivings.

You have to truly find out what each individual means when they say they want to submit to you! Many of course want to be ordained but don't want to submit to anyone... It's the apostles and the apostolic teams that connect the local churches which in effect stops any isolation of any individual group... i.e. we are one universal body...

Am I ordaining a ministry gift or an elder of the local church? Eldership is governmental, an office of responsibility with authority to rule. Each elder, as we have already seen, is a shepherd *(which does not mean that they are automatically a pastor)* and perhaps, will operate to some degree in their gifting. On the other hand we also then need to recognize that not every elder is a five fold ministry gift.

Submitting one to Another

Remembering, an apostolic ministry does have governmental authority. He can be responsible for a region, territory, nation, etc. Although the other five fold ministry gifts should submit to an apostle that they are in relationship with. They may have some governmental authority but it's meant to operate in submission to the apostolic structure.

As ministry gifts are not necessarily governmental positions, unless they are apostolic, but even then the apostle submits to the authority of the local church... We as apostles only have authority over any individual group as a result of submission through relationship. It is fundamental that the apostolic anointing that we are discussing here is *recognized.*

I only ordain leaders because I know them personally or leadership that is in relationship with me knows the person in question personally. The reason for this is that elders or ministry gifts for that matter *(when I mean ministry gifts, I mean itinerant ministries)* have to be qualified as seen in the New Testament. You cannot personally qualify an individual if you don't know them.

Therefore in the New Testament when elders were being put into a position of leadership, this was done by an apostle and presbytery of apostolic leaders. You will also find in the New Testament that there was an emphasis on elders being recognized by the people, the local body as good and honourable individuals. But once eldership has been appointed they then have the right to ordain anyone who God raises up to a position of elder or ministry gift in the local church *(as the local elders are the authority for their given territory)*. This can be approved by the apostle.

Ordination Service

Once all the above is clarified you then can set a date for the ordination service. This can be done in any given setting. I usually ordain ministers in front of their congregation because the congregation also needs to see that their pastor is submitting to an apostle. This would be a normal Sunday morning, perhaps one would teach on church structure or some other leadership message, referring to ordination. The body of Christ needs to understand what is going on...

Then at the right time, laying hands on the individual to recognize their position and praying for an impartation. This needs to be done with a presbytery of other leaders including other visiting pastors... Words of knowledge and encouragement are also important.

Expect the supernatural, change and increase not only for the minister in question but also for the church as the anointing should then increase. Again you can look at Acts 14:23, Titus 1:5. Even the apostle Paul told Timothy to fight the good fight using the word of prophecy given to him when hands were laid on him: 1 Timothy 1:18.

Regarding ongoing relationships, this is down to the type of relationship that you have agreed upon. Our role as apostles is to help father ministry gifts or elders to become the best that they can be. Watching as a father over their child who is trying to walk for the first time... applauding their victories... loving them enough to overlook their failures... Seeing their future success.

The Instruction of the Holy Spirit

There are many other issues that need to be observed but all that I know I have learned from the Holy Spirit. I have learned that many want to use the gift, which is fine, but I am not so quick to ordain people these days.

The given individual to be ordained has to pay for the traveling expenses, paper work that is incurred, honorarium on the day, and renew their membership fee every January. Why? This keeps them accountable... If however a Senior Pastor says he wants to be in affiliation then they have to tithe the tithe to me as their apostle.

Hope all this is helpful... Remember we don't wear nametags! People are trying to find out how to be an apostle... That is the wrong perspective on it... Whatever is in the bottle will be tasted when the bottle is poured out... You don't learn to be an apostle, you allow the apostle in you to be revealed!

Validating the Selection

As we know it was the apostles who validated the selections made by the people. Remarkably, these men were being given responsibility for what might be considered as a menial task, yet they were required to be full of the Holy Spirit and wisdom. One of the men, Stephen, described as being full of faith, grace and power *(verses 5 and 8)*, displayed signs and wonders befitting any apostle. So much so, that he incurred the wrath of the religious rulers who promptly persecuted him and contrived his death.

The fact that the first man ordained by the apostles should also be the first Christian martyr would indicate the spiritual importance of ordination. Were it to be of little spiritual value, it would not have drawn so much opposition. The pressure on the apostles to refrain from further ordination would have been considerable, *(i.e., "If this is what is going to happen when we ordain people, it doesn't seem like too good an idea!")*

Similarly, the pressure on individuals to hold back from being ordained to ministry would have been great. But then - those full of the Holy Spirit, faith, grace and power are not easily intimidated!

Ordination therefore is carried out by those appointed by God, whose authority is evidenced by the position of responsibility they hold within the body of Christ and by the demonstration of the Holy Spirit's power on their lives. *Such men (apostles) have something of value to impart.*

The Appointment and Ordination of Elders

In the early church, the appointment of elders was very important. In fact, the apostle Paul saw the church as *"unfinished"* until this happened *(Titus 1:5)*. The scriptures suggest that the elders were not selected by apostles or other trans-local ministries *(Acts 14:23; Titus 1:5)*, but were ordained, appointed or installed. It seems they ratified or confirmed the validity of the church's selection of men for the task and then *"officially"* appointed them.

In the new churches, which only had immature believers as members, the apostles *(or church planters)* had to help the church to recognise elders *(as the apostle Paul did when he described the qualifications for eldership)*. Note though that there is no place from scripture for the appointment of elders by democratic vote. It is God who calls, equips and enables elders, not the church members. The church has simply to recognise them, perhaps with apostolic help.

At first, the apostles *(and other trans-local ministries)* exercised authority in the church, *and* then later it was exercised by those they appointed as elders. The trans-local ministries never appointed men immediately a church was established, but appointed some members of the community to this position on subsequent *"missionary"* visits. This allowed time for some members of the new Christian community to mature sufficiently spiritually for others in the group to recognise this and their calling in God to be elders.

After all, there was no point appointing a person, as an elder if the majority of a congregation did not recognise them as such. Members of the congregation would also be able to test the people over time to see if they met the qualifications for eldership stressed by the apostle Paul. Note that elders in the early church were always drawn from the local community.

This meant that elders had to be members of the community, therefore enabling them to know the local situation and people intimately, and be able to make their judgements in the light of this as they carried out their oversight of the church.

Recognised as they Emerge

Men should never be appointed to eldership just because the church does not have elders or to make up the number of elders. Elders should only be recognised as they emerge. In some newly formed churches, it may be necessary to have a leadership, but not a properly constituted eldership. Elders will emerge later in God's time. This process must never be rushed. To end up with people appointed to eldership who are not called by God to the task can be devastating to a local church. Remember that a man is an elder before he is ever recognised as one, because it is a calling of God.

The requirements or qualifications for eldership will simply be met in Him and the church members must recognise this. This is the only way the man will be entrusted and therefore enable him to function as an elder. Note though that not all members of a church will be drawn to the same man for help and counsel etc. *(that is why God's best is plurality of eldership),* but most members of the flock need at least to be able to look up to and respect those chosen for eldership.

The number of elders recognised will usually be related to church size. God will not raise up ten elders in a church of twenty members. He will also not want one elder in a church of considerable size, as the job will be too great for one man alone. If, in a small church, only one man is recognisable as an elder, it would be wise for him to seek fellowship with other elders in his geographical area, where possible.

This will give him the opportunity to share his burdens and concerns with others and also be helped in his work. It is possible that the early church worked on this principle, as elders could have been appointed to geographical areas with each one overseeing one house-church.

Men should NOT be appointed as elders simply because:

- They are old. Remember though that spiritual maturity and wisdom do not develop overnight, so age is not entirely irrelevant
- They have served the church faithfully for many years
- They have successfully served in another area of church leadership for a number of years and they are due for a promotion
- They have influence, power, money, popularity, are successful, or professionally capable
- They are outgoing, outspoken, eloquent or good communicators
- There is no one else

CHAPTER 7

The Office of an Elder

S o let's get back to the teaching on the apostle in regard to those who are promoting the hierarchy of bishops as the top structure of the church. In order to refresh, the word bishop simply means **"elder."**

...I saw four and twenty elders sitting, clothed in white raiment; and they had on their heads crowns of gold.
(Revelation 4:4 KJV)

The word episkopos occurs five times in the NT: once of Christ *(1 Peter 2:25)* and in four places of "bishops" or "overseers" in local churches *(Acts 20:28; Philippians 1:1; 1 Timothy 3:2, Titus 1:7)*. The verb episkopeo occurs in Hebrews 12:15 *("watching")* and *(in some NT MSS)* 1 Peter 5:2 *("exercising the oversight")*.

A bishop then has "oversight of," he is an "overseer." 1 Peter 5:2 says, "Feed the flock of God which is among you, taking the oversight thereof" *(KJV)*. The Greek word for "oversight" is episkopeo, Strong's #G1983 - to oversee, to beware, to look diligently, take the oversight. Extra words given: direction *(about the times)*, have charge of, take aim at *(spy)*, regard, consider, take heed, look at *(on)*, mark.

Elders in the Old Testament

So to continue let's take a look at eldership now in both the New and Old Testaments.

The Hebrew word for elders: *zaqen, (OT)* does not necessarily mean an old man, but does imply one of maturity and experience *(Numbers 11:16)*. They were recognised as the highest authoritative body over the people. They acted as the religious representatives of the nation *(Jeremiah 19:1; Joel 1:14; 2:16)*.

As well as handling many political matters and settling inter tribal disputes *(Joshua 22:13-33)*, the town elders were a sort of municipal council, whose duties included acting as judges in apprehending murderers *(Deuteronomy 19:12)*, conducting inquests *(Deuteronomy 21:2)* and settling matrimonial disputes *(Deuteronomy 22:15; 25:7)*.

The *"elders of Israel,"* first heard of in Exodus 3:16-18, were assembled by Moses to receive God's announcement of the liberation of Egypt. The covenant was ratified at Mount Sinai in the presence of 70 elders of Israel *(Exodus 24:1,9,14 cf. 19:7)*, the *"nobles"* *(KJV)* or chief men of the nation *(24:11)*.

Later 70 elders were specially anointed with the Spirit to aid Moses in governing the nation *(Numbers 11:16-25)*. In cases when the whole community sinned, the elders of the congregation or community were to represent it in making atonement *(Leviticus 4:13-15)*.

The authority of the elders was in principle greater than that of the King *(cf, 2 Kings 23:1)*. It was this group, which demanded that Samuel appoint a king *(1 Samuel 8:4-6)*, and they were parties to the royal covenant, which established David as king *(2 Samuel 5:3)*.

In Babylon the elders were the focal point of the Jewish community in exile *(Jeremiah 29:1; Ezra 8:1; 14:1; 20:1-5)*, and after the return to Jerusalem they continued active *(Ezra 5:5, 9; 6:7-8, 14; 10:8, 14)*. While their authority was originally civil, **by New Testament times** the "elders of the people" *(presbyeroi tou laou)* shared with the chief priests the power of determining religious affairs and if necessary of expulsion from the synagogue.

Elders in the New Testament

An elder in the NT is really a bishop. In his vision of heaven, John saw 24 elders seated upon thrones surrounding the throne of God, clothed in white garments and wearing golden crowns *(Revelation 4:4)*. They fall down in worship and cast their crowns before God's throne *(4:10; cf. 11:16; 19:4)*, and with their harps and bowls of incense, symbolising the prayers of the saints, they sing a new song to the Lamb *(5:8-10)*.

As elders they represent God's people; their thrones and crowns symbolise a kingly role, while their acts of worship and the bowls of incense suggest a priestly function. Thus they seem to be the chief representatives of the redeemed as a kingdom of priestly function *(Revelation 1:6; cf. 20:6; 1 Peter 2:5, 9; Exodus 19:6).*

They used the same word for *elder* in the OT and the NT, but the content of the Christian elder's ministry has changed, for it now includes visitation of the sick *(James 5:14).*

Elders are vital components within the structure of the church, including the restoration of the apostolic.

Elders and the apostles must work together. NOT in a power struggle but in complete unison, consulting with one another - bringing stability and strength to the local church.

However it is true to say that as we begin to see the apostles and elders working together again like in the time of the early church, we are going to begin to see an **unleashing of God's** power - restored to the church - a power that this world will NOT be able to resist or refute!

Authority and Power go Hand in Hand

When perfect order is restored *(concerning authority in the local church)* there will no longer be any shortage of power - in the church of the living God.

Looking at the early church, where elders seemed to have been **responsible** for groups of house-churches, *(at that* *time there were no church buildings!)* elders were appointed to make sure these groups stayed on the right track spiritually. They exercised the greatest authority of all the members and brought a sense of the fatherhood of God to the local church, such as: faith, security, confidence and spiritual covering.

Elders were also meant to establish and maintain a family atmosphere, which enabled the flow of love between members. This enabled the Holy Spirit to move in power and enabled new converts to be *kept secure* after any evangelistic effort. This meant they had to speak with people personally and not rule by notes in the church newsletter.

Elders were overseers who had spiritual responsibility for local church members. It has already been stated: it was the elders and NOT the apostles - that ruled the local churches in New Testament times. Trans-local ministries such as apostles and prophets did at times bring some correction or exhortation, but the elders carried out their task of overseeing and shepherding the local church unhindered.

Leader of Leaders

From within a group of elders, God typically raises up a "set-elder" - a leader of leaders. This man is often the pastor, vicar, or full-time leader within a church. The elders may be of equal standing, but it would be very unusual for them all to be equal in leadership experience, gift and ability. The man who is called to lead the elders should enable eldership meetings by **"chairing"** them - in other words **"managing"** them and keeping them on the right track.

He is often also the spokesman for the eldership as well as being the main church teacher. Remember, every church member, including the elders, needs to submit to God and to any other person God raises up into a position of authority, i.e. an apostle bringing correction from God or a prophet bringing the "Word" of God. This submission to God and each other enables any church to be coordinated by God and fruitful as it seeks to carry out His will.

The scriptures do not reveal a clear job description for elders, but they do show us something of the way eldership functioned within the early church. Studying this can assist elders today in better understanding their significant role and what it is that God desires of them.

The qualifications we see in scripture concerning those serving in eldership - reveal the sheer **calibre and quality** of such men - chosen and expected to be fit for their task! These men had to serve the church to which they were called in a Christ-like way and other members of the church needed to recognize some measure of spiritual gifting and spiritual maturity in them.

For example those recognized, as elders should: direct the affairs of the church they were entrusted with by God, i.e. they were God's stewards *(Titus 1:1f; 1 Timothy 5:17)*. The Greek word for **"overseer"** is *episkopos* and was used in the secular writings of the time to refer to a person with **administrative and judicial functions.**

Therefore eldership is a governmental function, which has authority, and whose goal in the local church is to increase and maintain the rule of God; this affects each individual member, including their respective families, the church itself and the wider community.

Remember God never instituted "DEMOCRACY" as a means of governing His people. Rather He established "THEOCRACY" which means - government by God Himself. He enables His rule by raising up leadership - through whom He can rule *(principally eldership in a local church setting)*. These men therefore, must walk closely with God and wait on Him, so that they can hear His Word for the church for which they are responsible and obey His directives and take care of God's church.

They should also have a good reputation with those outside the church so that the church will be seen as a place of integrity, where non-Christians can come for help *(1 Timothy 3:5, 7)*. They also need to work hard, help the weak and remember that it is more blessed to give than receive *(Acts 20:35)*.

They must be able to Teach

The Greek word used here is ***didaktikos*** - better translated as "apt or skilled to teach" *(1 Timothy 3:2)*. However, 1 Timothy 5:17 suggests that only *some* had the labour *(or toil)* of preaching and teaching in the local church. This probably referred to those elders whose main function was preaching and teaching and perhaps even their full-time employment; hence the following verse about the worker deserving his wages *(1 Timothy 5:18)*.

All elders need to be able to teach and disciple *(even if it is just in a one-to-one counselling situation)*, however only some are called to preach and teach in a corporate sense.

Elders, when they are asked, anoint with oil in the name of the Lord those who are sick. The prayer offered in faith will make the sick person well, because the Lord will raise them up… *(James 5:14-15)* They also need to be on guard and watch over themselves and the flock of which the Holy Spirit has made them overseers/elders, because savage wolves will attempt to come in and will not spare the flock *(Acts 20:28-31)*.

In closing, elders are willing shepherds of the flock, that God has placed under their care - serving as **overseers** and **examples of Christ-likeness** to their flock *(Acts 20:28; 1 Peter 5:2-3)*. Their example should be Jesus Christ who is the **shepherd and overseer** of our souls *(1 Peter 2:25; 1 John 2:6)*.

Laying hands on and praying for those in their congregation, thus imparting spiritual gifts and prophecy *(1 Timothy 4:14)*. Encourage *(or exhort)* those they oversee by sound doctrine and by holding firmly to the trustworthy message as it has been taught, and refute *(or convict)* those who oppose it *(Titus 1:9)*.

Finally elders are to discern the truth of God in a given situation and guide the church for which they are responsible in the light of that truth.

The elders in Jerusalem did this with the apostles and therefore kept the church on the right path *(Acts 15:1-31; Acts 16:4)*.

❖

CHAPTER 8

Church Government

We were discussing the significance and the role of "elders" in both the Old and New Testaments. Specifically in the New Testament we saw that there was an addition to their function which was that of "visiting the sick" *(as seen in James 5:14)*. We also saw confirmed through scripture that elders appear to be the "chief representatives of the redeemed of the local church" and have a "...priestly function."

> *...They continued steadfastly in the apostles' doctrine and fellowship, and in breaking of bread, and in prayers.*
> *(Acts 2:42 KJV)*

However as we continue in light of the apostle, it was more in a *"corporate capacity"* by which he provided leadership for the primitive church; and that leadership was effective both in **mercy** *(Acts 2:42)* and in **judgment** *(Acts 5:1-11)*.

They exercised a general authority over every congregation, sending two of their number to supervise new developments in Samaria *(Acts 8:14)* and deciding with the elders on a common policy for the admission of Gentiles *(Acts 15)*. So in this context, we can see clearly, the apostles and elders working together for the benefit of the whole.

Pressure of Work

In Acts when the pressure of work increased, they appointed seven assistants *(Acts 6:1-6)*, elected by the people and ordained by the apostles. They were to administer to the churches charity. These seven have been regarded as deacons from the time of Irenaeus onwards, but Philip, the only one whose later history is clearly known to us, became an evangelist *(Acts 21:8)* with an unrestricted mission to preach the gospel. Church officers with a distinctive name are first found in the elders of Jerusalem, who received gifts *(Acts 11:30)* and took part in Council *(Acts 15:6)*.

This office was probably copied from the eldership of the Jewish synagogue. The church itself is called a synagogue in James 2:2 and Jewish elders, who seem to have been ordained by imposition of hands, were responsible for maintaining discipline, with power to excommunicate breakers of the law.

But Christian eldership, as a gospel ministry acquired added pastoral *(James 5:14; 1 Peter 5:1-3)* and preaching *(1 Timothy 1:5)*; and although the disturbances at Corinth may suggest that a more complete democracy prevailed in that congregation *(cf. 1 Corinthians 14:26)*, the general pattern of church government in the apostolic age would seem to be a board of elders or pastors. Possibly augmented by prophets and teachers, ruling each of the local congregations, with deacons to help in administration and with a general superintendence of the entire church **provided by apostles** *(not bishops!)*

Two Distinct Biblical Qualifications

The late Dr. Bob Gordon once wrote, "There are two biblical qualifications for eldership; these are distinct from others... **elders must not be novices and that they must be able to teach.** The other qualifications are a check to make sure that those proposed for eldership are living an exemplary Christian life. Those who are to oversee the church need to be good ambassadors for it, for Christ *(i.e. be models of Christlikeness)*, and for the truths they were teaching and not merely professional leaders.

Elders therefore need to be: men of prayer, true worshippers of God, men of the Word of God, men of true spiritual authority and maturity and men of mature spiritual experience and understanding. Men who are spiritually ahead of those in the church, men of vision *(which is sourced in God)*, who receive God's guidance and revelation and who are sensitive to the moving of the Holy Spirit; and men of faith, because without faith it is impossible to please God.

Elders are recognised by who they are and not what they do, and not by age or official title. They need to be men who have largely got their spiritual priorities right and their life in spiritual order.

The qualifications in the New Testament for an elder (*overseer*) are many:

- Shepherds of God's flock that is under their care, serving as overseers - not because they must, but because they are willing, as God wants them to be *(1 Peter 5:2)*

- Not greedy for money nor a lover of money *(1 Peter 5:2; 1 Timothy 3:3)*

- Eager to serve, of ready mind or willingly *(1 Peter 5:2)*

- Examples to their flock, not lording it over those entrusted to them *(1 Peter 5:3)*

- The husband of but one wife *(1 Timothy 3:2; Titus 1:6). (Note: divorce is allowable in scripture in certain circumstances; therefore, this phrase refers to bigamy or polygamy, not divorce)*

- A man whose children are faithful and not accused of riot or unruly *(Titus 1:6)*

- Blameless *(Titus 1:6-7)*

- Not overbearing *(not self-willed) (Titus 1:7)*

- Not quick tempered *(not soon angry) (Titus 1:7)*

- Not given to much wine *(1 Timothy 3:3: Titus 1:7)*

- Not violent *(no striker or brawler) (1 Timothy 3:3; Titus 1:7)*

- Not pursuing dishonest gain *(Titus 1:7)*

- Hospitable *(a lover of and given to hospitality) (Titus 1:8; 1 Timothy 3:2)*

- One who loves what is good *(Titus 1:8)*

- Self-controlled *(sober) (1 Timothy 3:2)*

- Upright *(just) (Titus 1:8)*

- Holy *(Titus 1:8)*

- Disciplined *(temperate) (Titus 1:8)*

- Able to hold firmly to the trustworthy message as it has been taught, so that they can encourage others by sound doctrine and refute those who oppose it *(Titus 1:9)*

- Above reproach *(1 Timothy 3:2)*

- Temperate *(vigilant) (1 Timothy 3:2)*

- Respectable *(of good behaviour) (1 Timothy 3:2)*

- Able *(apt or skilled)* to teach *(1 Timothy 3:2)*

- Not quarrelsome *(contentious or given to fighting) (1 Timothy 3:3)*

- Gentle *(patient) (1 Timothy 3:3)*

- Not covetous *(1 Timothy 3:3 AV)*

- Able to manage their own family well and see that their children obey them with proper respect... If anyone does not know how to manage *(rule)* their own family *(house),* how can they take care of God's church *(1 Timothy 3:4-5)*

- Not a recent convert *(a novice),* or they may become conceited *(puffed up with pride)* and fall under the same judgement as the devil *(1 Timothy 3:6)*

- Of good reputation with outsiders *(have a good testimony among those who are outside)*, so that they will not fall into disgrace and into the devil's trap *(lest they fall into reproach and the snare of the devil)* *(1 Timothy 3:7)*

- Able to work with other men in mutual submission, because they are called to work as an eldership team and not as individuals *(elders of a congregation are always mentioned in the plural)*

Important note: a true elder will tend the sheep whether recognised or not and will not want position or self-aggrandisement, but rather will simply want to serve the flock to which God has called him.

A man who starts to do this, but gives up because he was not recognised or officially appointed, proves that he is selfishly motivated. Such a man is not serving because 'he is called to the task by God' but is serving for his own gain rather than for the good of the church'" (Gordon 155-156).

❖

CHAPTER 9

Elders are Territorial

As we continue with this concept of the apostle, we have taken the last chapters along with this one to talk about the role of elders in the body of Christ, in yester-world and in today's-world. All authority has "influence" - and all influence has a "realm of influence" over which it operates.

> *Remember your leaders who have spoken God's Word to you. Think about how their lives turned out, and imitate their faith.*
>
> *(Hebrews 13:7 GW)*

Now we are going to look at this in terms of the world territory. So let's begin by looking at what this word **"territory"** actually means. Its literal meaning is as follows: **"an area regarded as owned by the state, social group, individual or animal."**

In addition to this, another significant word that describes territory is "province," which in times-past was the basic **"unit of administration"** within the Roman Empire. Its earliest usage was a general term that referred to the **"magistrate's sphere of administrative action."** This term signified both the **"rule"** of the governor and the **"region"** that was entrusted to his care *(the geographical sense was dominant)*; and included the **"administration of justice."**

Therefore when a province was given to a governor, this was for him to: control, supervise, protect and oversee. It literally became his territory - to rule and to govern - for a specific period of time.

Elders are Territorial

Now when it comes to the spiritual aspect of this matter - there are such things as **"territorial spirits"** *(which are active within the heavenly realms)* but this is another teaching altogether! However as believers it is our right to exercise our authority within any given territory and we too are meant to be territorial!

We are not merely undercover agents that live invisible to the world, with alter egos that no one knows about! We are not a secret society! Rather we ought to govern those areas or regions that God has entrusted to us as scripture speaks about - holding-claim to every place we put our feet! *(see "Territorial Spirits" by C. Peter Wagner)*

This is too general in thought, even though all believers possess authority to a degree - not all believers are called to governmental offices - such as elders and apostles for example. So we must not over generalise this issue. Now let's go beyond this and look more closely at our opening chapter title **"Elders are Territorial."**

This statement refers to the fact that God placed elders within the church to oversee it. Their influence was not merely for the church only, but regionally and spiritually *(in the spirit realm)*. Their influence is far reaching both practically and spiritually. For instance if we go to the Old Testament, we can see that elders often acted as "magistrates" and "judges," who represented the people. Therefore it was their job to "administrate justice" within the areas allocated to them.

Even today this whole structure has NOT changed - because of time! Rather it still continues today; the only thing that has changed is that elders today have the added responsibility of visiting and praying for the sick. They do so in the power of the name of Jesus and His blood!

Elders also represent "pillars" within the church: of maturity, wholeness, purity, integrity, righteousness, doctrine and all that is true.

Every church needs Good Elders!

How then should the church respond to such elders? Well firstly there are three major things that need to be noted from scripture.

Firstly: elders are worthy of double honour, especially those whose work is preaching and teaching *(1 Timothy 5:17)*.

Church members need to respect, uphold and admonish them *(1 Thessalonians 5:12-13).*

The job of an elder is not easy and the church needs to encourage those who are overseeing them and not pull them down or make their job more difficult than it needs to be. In fact, church members should obey their elders and submit to their authority, because they are men who keep watch over the church and who are accountable before God for it *(Hebrews 13:17).* Also, if an elder is serving the church on a full-time basis, then the scriptures tell us that the worker deserves his wages *(1 Timothy 5:18).*

Secondly: church members should not entertain an accusation against an elder unless it is brought by two or three witnesses.

Elders do not need to be the subject of gossip, which only serves to undermine their credibility and authority. Members of the church should stop people who do this and stop something getting out of hand or being blown out of proportion to the truth. However, if an elder is found to be in sin, they are to be rebuked publicly, so that others may take warning *(1 Timothy 5:19-20).*

Thirdly: the church members should follow the godly example set by the elders *(Hebrews 13:7).*

We all know that scripture tells us to "seek first the kingdom of God." The word kingdom also represents the **"rule and reign"** of God in scripture. But now we look at the role of elders as they use their God given positions to reign, to rule and to exercise Godly authority wherever they are placed. They actually represent the government of God within the church and must act accordingly.

All of this ties in with the role of the apostle and the apostolic age. The elders do not function under their own authority nor do the apostles. All authority given by God must work together in unity not in contest or rivalry with each other. A house divided falls. It cannot stand and until the elders can work together with the apostles in the local church as they were ordained and equipped to do so, there will always be a certain lack of authority and power.

So bring it on! Bring on the order of God. The church is in need of her power. She needs to be stifled no longer. Let truth be taught and revelation restored to the body of Christ. As all man-made-efforts to rule and to govern, have left her barren and lacking powerful influence within society. But if she regains her position and spiritual possession - with all her dignity in tact - the world will learn once again, what it is to FEAR the authority of the living God - that exists within the local church!

Awesome Authority has Responsibility

Finally, in closing this chapter - my son who is now 21 years, got talking to his mother about the story in the bible of Ananias and Sapphire. They were discussing the awesome authority that the apostles exercised in the early church. However over lunch our son came up with this honest and simple question *(and I quote him word for word simply because I think others would ask the same question!)*: **"If the apostle is being 'restored' where did he go? What happened to him?"**

This legitimate question was deserving of a simple reply! "The fact of the matter is…" I told him, "The apostle never went anywhere! He is not the one being restored, rather the truth about his *role* is being restored to the body of Christ." "Why?" "Because over time, truth was replaced by deception and distortion."

When TRUTH is fully restored to the church *(before Christ returns)* via the revealed Word of God *(the teaching of "revelation")* the apostle will be able to take his rightful place, along with the elders. No longer stuffy relics of an age-old institute or relegated to stain-glass-windows of rotting church buildings. No! They will not remain this ineffective but will take their rightful places in their intended role as POWERFUL EXECUTORS OF GOD'S AUTHORITY & JUSTICE.

The government of God within the local church is vital. The apostle has a huge part to play in this, along with the elders.

May this RESTORATION OF TRUTH advance with speed! How the church needs her divine order - just as God planned it and not as man distorted it - by humanistic ideals and religious **replacement theology!**

CHAPTER 10

Women in Ministry

The apostle Paul clearly states that in God's eyes there is no distinction between male and female.

You are all sons of God through faith in Christ Jesus, for all of you who were baptised into Christ have clothed yourself with Christ. There is neither Jew nor Greek, slave nor free, male nor female, for you are all in Christ Jesus.

(Galatians 3:26-28)

The same man instructed Timothy *(1 Timothy 2:11-14)* that the order of headship between man and woman, irrespective of spiritual equality in God's eyes, must be upheld *(Galatians 3:28)*. He did not permit a woman to teach or have authority over a man.

The statement does not prohibit a woman from teaching in general terms but rather, taking the headship belonging to the man.

They are Significant

Throughout scripture there are accounts of women who have played significant roles within God's order and plan. **Miriam** *(Exodus 15:20)*, **Deborah** *(Judges 4:14)*, **Huldah** *(2 Kings 22:14)*, **Noadiah** *(Nehemiah 6:14)*. **Esther** was ordained by God to be given within a foreign reign and used greatly to bring in reformation at that time.

There were many women who surrounded Jesus and who were significantly involved with His life in one way or another:

Anna, the prophetess spoke of Him, those who travelled with Him, those who ministered to Him, the last ones at the cross, and the first at the tomb, the first to announce the resurrection (Luke 2:36-38; Matthew 27:55-56; Luke 8:1-3; Mark 14:3; Luke 7:37-37; Mark 15:47; John 20:1; Matthew 28:8).

Jesus never expressed discouragement concerning women and ministry, far from it! The woman Jesus spoke to at the well *(John 4:1-26)* was used by the Holy Spirit to evangelise her hometown.

The evangelist Philip is recorded to have had daughters who prophesied *(Acts 21:9)*. For this information to be included in the Word of God it must have significance beyond that of what Paul spoke in *1 Corinthians 12:7-11*.

God is Not Averse to Promoting Women

History gives record also to the fact that God is not averse to *"promoting"* women to high places of ministry within the body of Christ. Kathryn Kuhlman was a woman mightily anointed by God and her ministry outshines that of many men. She is reported as saying that the reason God used her was because a number of men refused to take the mantle of anointing, so because she was willing God used her. This statement may have considerable credibility but the fact remains – God used her.

She appears to reflect Deborah the prophetess in many ways. Deborah tried to encourage Barak to take the initiative in dealing with their enemy. Because he wouldn't, Deborah prophesied that the glory or credit would go to a woman. This was exactly what happened, *(Judges 4-5)* and it wasn't even Deborah!

Governmental Authority

There is no doubt that God's plan is for the men to carry that responsibility. Adam was created first therefore he had the responsibility and initial relationship with God. Aside from this the physical and emotional differences between man and woman confirm the wisdom of God's order. He created hormones and therefore knew exactly how they would affect the emotional balance of an individual.

God said that the woman's desire would be for her husband and that he would rule over her *(Genesis 3:16)*. Peter talks about women being submissive to their husbands

(1 Peter 3:1-6). It is quite clear therefore that should a woman be looking for position above her husband or striving for equality *(in the wrong sense),* then this is not of God.

This however does not prevent women from having prominent ministries that flow out from a marriage relationship. The key is found in the heart attitude and submission, primarily to the Lord and then to the husband.

Can a woman be a five fold ministry gift? Can she be a pastor? Can she be an evangelist? Can she be a prophetess? Can she be an apostle, a pioneer or leader?

The answer to each of these questions would have to be, **YES.**

Can a woman be a man? **NO.**

❖

CHAPTER 11

Mandate for Fellowship with God's Spirit

It is so important in this last chapter to strongly encourage you to **cultivate a deep and *daily* fellowship with the Holy Spirit.** Knowing that when it comes to fellowship with Him, it is vitally important to have a firm understanding of just whom we are relating to. He is not a mystical being for instance, but a distinct person, namely the third person of the trinity.

> ...when the **Friend** comes, the Spirit of the Truth, **he** will take you by the hand and guide you into all the truth there is. **He** won't draw attention to **himself**, but will make sense out of what is about to happen and, indeed, out of all that I have done and said. **He** will honor me; **he** will take from me and deliver it to you...
>
> (John 16:13 MSG)

As we develop an apostolic lifestyle let's look at what the Spirit does - this will aid us in our grasp of who He really is and how we can relate to Him in our walk and ministries. I have continual mentioned, *"LifeStyle"* or *"daily"* throughout these pages, simply because our fellowship with the Holy Spirit is something that we should pursue daily.

Actually there is much about the Lord in scripture that is "daily" such as: "daily bread" *(Matthew 6:11)*, "fresh manna every morning" *(Exodus 16:21)*, "mercy is new every day" *(Lamentations 3:22-23)*, "take up our cross daily" *(Luke 9:23)* and so forth. Why? Because when something is "living" it is always a "daily experience."

Keeping it daily helps keeping it Fresh!

Bread is predominantly associated with scripture and is something, which for the most part, goes particularly stale after just one day! Same too concerning our relationship with the Holy Spirit, we must keep it fresh. In fact everything about our relationship with God must be kept fresh - not stale, stuffy or religious! We achieve this by approaching Him and welcoming Him afresh - every single day.

This daily pursuit is a journey of discovery that changes our personality in the process. So why don't more people in general try it, what is their cramp? One obvious hurdle that folks have grappled with is the fact that unlike Jesus *(who we saw dwelt amongst us)*, people can't see the Spirit of God with "flesh and bones" *(John 1:14; Luke 24:39)*. This single difficulty throughout church history has led some to either ignore the Spirit completely in their day-to-day Christian lives or keep Him as some kind of spiritual spare tire for emergencies only.

However it is only a sheer lack of understanding that can be the culprit here, for such neglect of this significant member of the Trinity. For example scripture certifies that we are born of the Spirit *(John 3:6)* and that our bodies are the temple of the Holy Spirit - who indwells us, *(Romans 8:9, 11, 14-16)* and that His witness gives us assurance that we are children of God. Also we are baptized by one Spirit into the body of Christ and we have access to God by the same Spirit *(1 Corinthians 12:13; Ephesians 2:14).*

With all this in mind - who would willingly dare to be so casual or caviler in their attitude towards the Holy Spirit? Ignorance can be the only cause; including deception and false teaching that has always dogged and hindered believers in their perception of Him. Our adversary works overtime to ensure this dull perception, knowing better than we just how potent we would be if fully surrendered to the Holy Spirit.

There is a huge difference throughout church history between Christians who walked with the Holy Spirit and those who didn't - quite simply they lacked essential power! Still today we have a choice whether to be "thrilled, filled, or spilled." In other words, mere excitement *(being thrilled)* counts for nothing compared to being fully surrendered *(filled)* and used *(spilled)* by Him!

Nevertheless those who struggle to know the Holy Spirit personally are chiefly those who struggle to see Him as a personality. It is usually the religious folks who have the most difficulty with this!

Nevertheless a definition of personality *(on a human level at least)* refers in general to a complexity of attributes such as; behavioural, temperamental, emotional and mental - that help characterize the uniqueness of an individual. Whereas a more simple definition of personality refers to "person-like-qualities," such as: the ability to talk and to listen (*a.k.a. "the ability to communicate"*) to think and to reason; to feel and to have emotions; decision-making and free will.

Personality unmistakably Verified

When broken down like this - especially in reference to the Holy Spirit - it becomes abundantly clear that He does indeed have a person-ality - that of which is unmistakably verified throughout scripture.

For example: Jesus and Paul both continually referred to the Holy Spirit as "He," not "It" (*John 14:16, 17, 26; 15:26; 16:7, 8, 13, 14*). Then our opening scripture refers continually to His "personage" John 16:13; "Howbeit when **He**, the Spirit of truth, is come, **He** will guide you into all truth: for **He** shall not speak of **Himself**; but whatsoever **He** shall hear, that shall **He** speak: and **He** will show you things to come. **He** shall glorify Me..."

Luke 2:26 sees Him "speaking" to man, "...it was revealed unto him by the Holy Ghost" and in various scriptures from both Old and New Testaments, specific qualities of His character are well pointed out: **Goodness** (Nehemiah 9:20; Galatians 5:22, 23); **Holiness** (Romans 1:4); **Truth** (John 14:17; 15:26; 16:13); **Grace** (Hebrews 10:29; Zechariah 12:10); **Comfort** (John 14:26; 15:26); **Patience, Love, Gentleness**, etc. (Galatians 5:22, 23).

Most significantly the Holy Spirit is "one with God" *(Isaiah 48:16; Matthew 28:19; Acts 5:3, 4; 1 Corinthians 3:16; 6:19; 12:4-6; 2 Corinthians 13:14; 1 John 5:7)*. Therefore He has all the attributes of God - He is eternal *(Hebrews 9:14)*. He was present with God in the creation of the world *(Genesis 1:2, 3; Job 26:13; 33:4; Psalms 104:30)*. He is "omnipresent" *(Psalms 139:7-10)*. He is "omniscient" *(Isaiah 40:13; 1 Corinthians 2:10, 11)*. He is "omnipotent" *(Psalms 104:30)*.

Yet He is a distinct personality apart from both the Father and the Son. Besides that, scripture uses many types of symbols to describe His many functions and responsibilities including many Old Testament scriptures that identify Him *(Isaiah 11:2; 42:1; 48:16; 61:1; 63:9; Ezekiel 36:26, 27)*. So as far as scripture is concerned the Holy Spirit is undeniably a "personality" and a very powerful one at that!

The Crux of Problem

Consequently those who lack revelation of God's Word will be the ones who struggle to relate to Him. They will posses limited perception of who the Spirit of God is; for example an impersonal "power" or "force" such as electricity!

This impersonal view of Him is the crux of their problem. And while there are "mystical" and "ancient philosophies" that present a plethora of "counterfeit-personalities" for folks to "relate to" - they are no more than cleverly designed plans that appeal to the "spiritual curiosity" of millions who are completely distracted and beguiled from the real McCoy.

Every believer however must eliminate any obstacle that hinders their fellowship with the Holy Spirit and not be duped by religious doctrines or the infiltration of worldly philosophies - which are equally misleading!

For instance it could be said that mainline evangelical Christianity has no problem with the doctrine of the Trinity but their challenge comes with this issue of relating to the Holy Spirit on a personal level. Until this is resolved, fellowship with Him will always be disputed; meaning that many will fail to give Him the place that He truly deserves. The Word and the Holy Spirit must be working in conjunction in our lives, without which we have no revelation and our endeavours will be Godless!

To continue, both Old and New Testaments report the work of the Spirit extensively. "This is the word of the LORD to Zerubbabel: 'Not by might nor by power, but by My Spirit,' says the LORD of hosts" *(Zechariah 4:6 NKJV)*.

> *I will pour out My Spirit on all flesh; your sons and your daughters shall prophesy, your old men shall dream dreams, your young men shall see visions. And also on my menservants and on My maidservants I will pour out My Spirit in those days.*
>
> *(Joel 2:28-29 NKJV)*

Jesus was anointed with the Holy Spirit *(Acts 10:38)* and led by the Spirit to be tempted by Satan and returned in the power of the Spirit *(Luke 4:1-2, 14)*. Jesus cast out evil spirits by the Holy Spirit *(Matthew 12:28)*.

In fact, it would not be incorrect to suggest that the entire ministry of our Lord, was influenced by and "one" with the anointing of the Holy Spirit. Jesus Himself qualified this by saying,

The Spirit of the Lord is upon me, because he hath anointed me to preach the gospel to the poor; he hath sent me to heal the broken hearted, to preach deliverance to the captives, and recovering of sight to the blind, to set at liberty them that are bruised, To preach the acceptable year of the Lord.
(*Luke 4:18-19 KJV*)

Once we master this continual fellowship with the Holy Spirit, as believers we will also enjoy the intimate bond of fellowship, which binds us together in Christ. There is also fellowship with the Father and the Son as seen here in 1 John 1:3 AMP,

What we have seen and [ourselves] heard, we are also telling you, so that you too may realize and enjoy fellowship as partners and partakers with us. And [this] fellowship that we have [which is a distinguishing mark of Christians] is with the Father and with His Son Jesus Christ (the Messiah).

Then also in 1 Corinthians 1:9 it speaks of specific fellowship with the Son; "God is faithful (*reliable, trustworthy, and therefore ever true to His promise, and He can be depended on*); by Him you were called into companionship and participation with His Son, Jesus Christ our Lord."

One yet Three

However as ONE yet THREE - Father, Son and Spirit - remain very distinct personalities. Even though our fellowship is with all of them our emphasis remains the Holy Spirit and the following list of sins that are directly hostile to the person and ministry of the Holy Spirit, must be avoided by anyone seeking to cultivate a genuine fellowship with Him.

- **Grieving Him:** (Ephesians 4:30) by adopting behaviour contrary to the fruits; bitterness, unforgiveness, etc.

- **Quenching Him:** (1 Thessalonians 5:19) by disallowing the gifts and anointing to work through our lives

- **Insulting Him:** (Hebrews 10:29) through deliberate sin even after receiving knowledge of truth

- **Resisting Him:** (Acts 7:51) going in the opposite direction to the definite guidance of the Spirit

- **Vexing Him:** (Isaiah 63:10) through intentional rebellion against His leadership

- **Lying to Him:** (Acts 5:3) by speaking untruths to His anointed men and women in order to deceive

- **Testing Him:** (Acts 5:9) by provoking Him into action - not out of faith but out of fear

- **Blaspheming Him:** (Matthew 12:31, 32) by attributing the things of Him to demons

- **Striving with Him:** (Genesis 6:3) by walking in the flesh continually against His promptings

- **Rebelling against Him:** (Psalms 106:33) by refusing His instructions

As believers our lives are supernatural. Our fallen natures continue to rage against us *(Galatians 5:16; Romans 7:14-22)* and therefore we continually need to be empowered from within and above in order to live and walk worthy of our calling.

Our Lord explained that the Spirit will guide us into all truth and give us ability to cope with life and its stresses.

With a cultivated lifestyle that is one with Him, we can avoid doctrinal pitfalls and the trickery of our adversary by trusting our "Paraclete" to outwit him *(1 Peter 5:8; John 16:12-13).*

Sensitivity comes via spending time in His presence and is the only way that we can gain firsthand knowledge and gain the skills of detection that we need concerning what grieves and pleases Him moment by moment. Gradually we experience growth in all these areas, the awkwardness flees and a fluent relationship emerges with maturity.

Finally possibly most importantly, as we have an "abandoned devotion" towards God's Word - devouring scripture and making it the final word on every issue - also means that we will always respect the authority of the Spirit who never speaks or gives instruction contrary to the Word.

All in all we eventually find ourselves enjoying His company above all else which finally determines that we have cultivated such a passion for Him, that counts the passions of this world as dung! *(Philippians 3:8)*

❖
Bibliography

- Bevere, John. <u>Thus Saith the Lord?</u> Copyright © 1999. Published by Creation House, A Division of Strang Communications Company. Printed in USA.

- Ekman, Ulf. <u>The Prophetic Ministry</u>. Copyright © 1990. Published by Word of Life Publications. Printed in Sweden.

- Gordon, Bob, and David Fardouly. <u>Master Builders</u>. Copyright © 1990. Published by Sovereign World. Printed in England.

- Hamon, Bill. <u>Apostles, Prophets and the Coming Moves of God</u>. Copyright © 1997. Published by Destiny Image Publishers, Inc. Printed in USA.

- Mohabir, Philip. <u>Hands of Jesus</u>. Copyright © 2003. Published by Powerhouse Publishing. Printed in Denmark.

- Strong, James. S.T.D., L.L.D. 1890. <u>Strong's Exhaustive Concordance; Dictionaries of the Hebrew and Greek Words</u>. e-Sword ® version 7.6.1 Copyright © 2000-2005. All Rights Reserved. Registered trade mark of Rick Meyers. Equipping Ministries Foundation. USA www.e-sword.net.

- Unless otherwise indicated, all scriptural quotations are from the HOLY BIBLE, NEW INTERNATIONAL VERSION ®. NIV ®. Copyright © 1973, 1978, 1984 by the International

❖

Ministry Profile

Doctor Alan Pateman, an apostle, is the President and Founder of **"Alan Pateman Ministries International"** (APMI), which was established in England back in 1987, a Christian-based *(parachurch)* non-profit and non-denominational outreach. This ministry is now focusing in two main areas: First **"Connecting for Excellence"** Apostolic Networking (CFE) and secondly, the teaching arm, **"LifeStyle International Christian University"** (LICU).

CFE is a multi-facetted missions organisation with the purpose of connecting leaders for divine opportunities and building lasting relationships, to touch the lives of leaders literally the world over. Apostle Dr Alan Pateman has to date ordained more than 500 ministers in over 50 NATIONS. In addition there are ministries, churches and schools who are in Association or Affiliation, looking to him for apostolic counsel and oversight.

Secondly LICU, which was founded in 2007, is a study program to help people discover their purpose and destiny. A global network of university campuses and correspondence students, demonstrating the Supernatural Kingdom of God through Doctrinal, Apostolic and Prophetic Teaching. Dr Alan holds the position of President/CEO, Professor of Theology, Biblical Studies and Apostolic Ministry. LICU is exploding throughout Europe, Asia and Africa, enhancing the Body of Christ

Dr Alan has authored more than 35 books including numerous teaching materials and LICU university courses (30) along with hundreds of Truth for the Journey articles on kingdom lifestyle *(that are regularly distributed globally via the internet).*

He is recognised as an Apostle, Bishop, Leadership Mentor, University Educator, Motivational Speaker, Connector and Author, who has also been featured on national and international TV and radio networks throughout the years.

Currently Apostle Alan, his wife Dr Jennifer reside in Lucca *(Tuscany)* Italy and travel out from their Apostolic Company.

- Alan Pateman Ph.D., D.Min., D.D., M.A., B.Th.

Academic Background

Dr. Alan Pateman attended several colleges throughout his training *(including studying Theology at Roffey Place, Horsham, UK and a Member of Kerygma - with Rev. Colin Urquhart and Dr. Bob Gordon - 1985-1987)* before being awarded a Doctorate of Divinity *(2006)* in recognition of his lifetime achievements by the International College of Excellence, now "DanEl Christian College" *(President: Dr. Robb Thompson USA)* also "Life Christian University" *(Dr. Douglas Wingate USA)* where he also earned a Bachelor of Theology B.Th. *(2006),* a Master of Arts in Theology M.A., a Doctor of Ministry in Theology D.Min., *(2007)* and Doctor of Philosophy in Theology Ph.D. *(2013)* from LICU.

❖

To Contact the Author

Please email:

Alan Pateman Ministries International

Email: apostledr@alanpateman.com
Web: www.AlanPatemanMinistries.com

*Please include your prayer requests
and comments when you write.*

❖

Other Books

Media, Spiritual Gateway

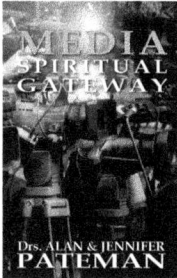

Let's face it; we live in the era of fake news! It's always existed, but never been quite so prominent. Today it's an all-out-war between fact and political fiction.

ISBN: 978-1-909132-54-2, Pages: 192, Format: Paperback, Published: 2018
Also available in eBook format!

Millennial Myopia, From a Biblical Perspective

The standard for every generation is Jesus. However Millennial Myopia describes the trap of focusing everything on one particular generation or demographic cohort, at the exclusion and expense of all others. The Church cannot afford to make this mistake too.

ISBN: 978-1-909132-67-2, Pages: 216, Format: Paperback, Published: 2017
Also available in eBook format!

Truth for the Journey Books

TONGUES, Our Supernatural Prayer Language

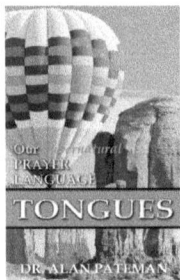

In writing to the church at Corinth, Paul encouraged them to continue the practice of speaking with other tongues in their worship of God and in their prayer lives as a means of spiritual edification. "He that speaketh in an unknown tongue edifies, charges, builds himself up like a battery."

ISBN: 978-1-909132-44-3, Pages: 144,
Format: Paperback, Published: 2016
Also available in eBook format!

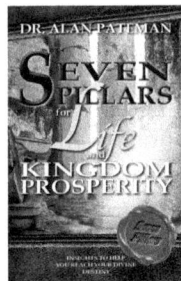

Seven Pillars for Life and Kingdom Prosperity

I submit these "Seven Pillars for Life and Kingdom Prosperity" to you, (Love, Prayer, Righteousness, Obedience, Connections, Management, Money). It's my desire that you walk in the triumphs that God has ordained for you.

ISBN: 978-1-909132-46-7, Pages: 220,
Format: Paperback, Published: 2016
Also available in eBook format!

Seduction & Control: Infiltrating Society & the Church

This book is a glance into the world of seduction and control, how they try to influence the Church through many powerful avenues such as the New Age, sexual education in our schools, basic entertainment; things that touch our everyday lives in order that we effectively and gradually become desensitised.

ISBN: 978-1-909132-00-9, Pages: 156
Format: Paperback, Published: 2015
Also available in eBook format!

Truth for the Journey Books

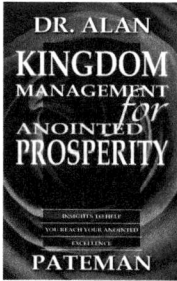

Kingdom Management for Anointed Prosperity

In his book, "Kingdom Management for Anointed Prosperity," Dr. Alan Pateman reveals how we can avoid living in continual crisis due to mismanagement. Life happens to all of us, but how we handle it matters most.

ISBN: 978-1-909132-34-4, Pages: 144, Format: Paperback, Published: 2015
Also available in eBook format!

Why War: A Biblical Approach to the Armour of God and Spiritual Warfare

Spiritual warfare means different things to different people, but from a biblical standpoint Ephesians 6:10-18 gives us the best biblical definition of spiritual warfare possible. We can also see how God has thoroughly equipped us for victory not just self defence!

ISBN: 978-1-909132-39-9, Pages: 180, Format: Paperback, Published: 2013
Also available in eBook format!

Forgiveness, The Key to Revival

Scripture is absolute when it comes to forgiveness. IF we forgive, THEN we are forgiven. It's that simple but no one said it was easy! Nonetheless, forgiveness can be likened to a spiritual key that unlocks spiritual doors and opportunities!

ISBN: 978-1-909132-41-2, Pages: 124, Format: Paperback, Published: 2013
Also available in eBook format!

Truth for the Journey Books

Revival Fires - Anointed Generals
Past & Present (Part Two of Four)

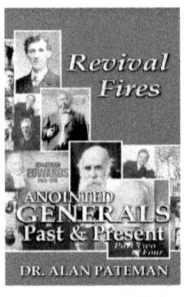

Seasons might be changing but God's Word remains the same. The heart of the author is to help train, equip and be a blessing to those men and women who will be willing to fulfil their potential in ministry and be properly equipped for service.

ISBN: 978-1-909132-36-8, Pages: 142, Format: Paperback, Published: 2012
Also available in eBook format!

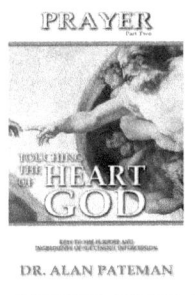

Prayer, Touching the Heart of God (Part Two)

Touching the Heart of God is the very essence of prayer. Whether we are petitioning God with very specific requests or consecrating ourselves before Him and rededicating our lives - whatever the case may be – the true essence of all praying is "Touching the Heart of God."

ISBN: 978-1-909132-12-2, Pages: 180, Format: Paperback, Published: 2012
Also available in eBook format!

Prayer, Ingredients for Successful Intercession
(Part One)

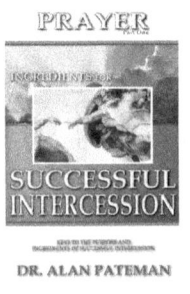

This Book is the first of two books on Prayer. Dr. Pateman provides an exhaustive study, showcasing the vital ingredients necessary for all successful prayer. An excellent power-packed teaching tool, either for the individual or for the local church prayer group, that's eager to lay a solid foundation but don't know where to start!

ISBN: 978-1-909132-11-5, Pages: 140, Format: Paperback, Published: 2012
Also available in eBook format!

Truth for the Journey Books

Apostles: Can the Church Survive Without Them?

Before Jesus returns a significant increase of the anointing will be poured out on the Body of Christ, but can the Church handle such an anointing? *(Acts 5:5)* Billy Brim once said, "As much as the anointing is powerful to create, it is as powerfully destructive of evil." The fear of God will be restored with the apostolic and people will begin walking with such anointing, as we have never seen before!

ISBN: 978-1-909132-04-7, Pages: 164,
Format: Paperback, Published: 2012
Also available in eBook format!

Sexual Madness: In a Sexually Confused World

This book discusses the sensitive subject of political correctness in our world today and the growing fear of causing offence in the public arena. It also discusses the rise of homosexuality, pedophilia and all other forms of sexuality, as there are many. Including modern statistics on pornography.

ISBN: 978-1-909132-02-3, Pages: 160,
Format: Paperback, Published: 2012
Also available in eBook format!

His Life is in the Blood

Blood is the trophy of every battle. The spilt blood of Jesus Christ is our trophy. It is our freedom from sin and bondage. Nothing can enter the blood-bought temples of the Holy Ghost! This book will encourage you to apply the blood of Jesus our Passover Lamb to your life, just as the children of Israel did in the Old Testament. Not merely talking or reading about it, but applying it.

ISBN: 978-1-909132-06-1, Pages: 152,
Format: Paperback, First Published: 2007
Also available in eBook format!

Truth for the Journey Books

WINNING by Mastering your Mind

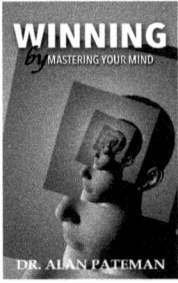

Someone once said, "Happiness begins between your ears and your mind is the drawing room for tomorrow's circumstances..." Remember, what happens in your mind will happen in time, and therefore one of our first priorities must be mind-management.

ISBN: 978-1-909132-40-5, Pages: 136,
Format: Paperback, Published: 2017
Also available in eBook format!

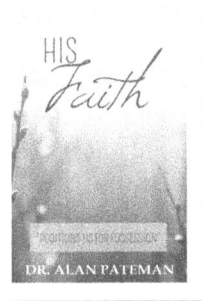

His Faith Positions us for Possession

It is with both simplicity and seasoned proficiency that Dr. Pateman draws us into this weighty conclusion; ...only as we yield and surrender to Christ's faith IN us – will we truly be empowered to live as Christ lived on this earth, "...as he is, so are we in this world" *(1 John 4:17)*.

ISBN: 978-0-9570654-0-6, Pages: 128,
Format: Paperback, Published: 2014
Also available in eBook format!

Dear Friends,

Have you considered becoming one of our international students? We are privileged to welcome you, from around the world, to "LifeStyle International Christian University" *(the teaching arm of Alan Pateman Ministries International).* **An English speaking university** dedicated to your success; to see you trained and equipped to fully succeed in your God given Destiny.

It is our passion to raise up the leaders of tomorrow, who will have influence in all realms of authority, including the Body of Christ. Men and women of strategy, wisdom and true godliness, who'll stand with stature and maturity in this hour.

It's undeniable that in today's world, recognised education has become indispensable, therefore it is our desire to offer well balanced and well structured courses. Those that have been written by gifted and talented ministers of God, who seek to be inspired by God's Holy Spirit.

Consequently we have put together a **flexible curriculum,** designed both for correspondence students and campuses, which is a strategy to reach the distant learner; whether provincial, national or international. In fact we have many correspondence students from around the world, including a growing number of successful campuses, in various countries.

This is a growing platform, where men and women of dignity and passion, can grow and be established in their God given endeavours. As God is the healer of the nations, we pray and believe that many of our alumni will go on to **become world changers** in their own right.

We are proud of each and every one of our LICU students.
It would be our pleasure if you would join them on this incredible journey!

Doctor Alan Pateman

Alan Pateman Prof. Ph.D., D.Min., D.D., M.A., B.Th.
PRESIDENT AND CEO
www.licuuniversity.com www.cfeapostolicnetwork.com
Email: info@licuuniversity.com Mob: +39 366 329 1315

For more information visit our website/facebook or contact our office, using the details below:

Website: www.licuuniversity.com
Facebook: www.facebook.com/LICUMainCampus
Email: info@licuuniversity.com
Telephone: +39 366 329 1315

All Books Available

at

APMI PUBLICATIONS

Email: publications@alanpateman.com
*Also Available from Amazon.com
and other retail outlets.*

*If you purchased this book through Amazon.com or
other and enjoyed reading it, or perhaps one of my
other books, I would be grateful if you could take
a couple of minutes to write a Customer Review,
many thanks.*

www.ingramcontent.com/pod-product-compliance
Lightning Source LLC
Chambersburg PA
CBHW071559040426
42452CB00008B/1223